Praise for *Playlist Judaism*

"A thoughtful examination of the historic, social, cultural, and demographic factors eroding today's synagogues and Jewish institutions, Playlist Judaism offers tools and strategies to guide these organizations in reshaping themselves to regain strength and vitality. Rabbi Olitzky provides a valuable perspective for synagogue change leaders seeking to transform the Jewish communal landscape of the 21st century."
— Rabbi Rick Jacobs, president, Union for Reform Judaism

"Synagogues are paralyzed when leaders are afraid of change. But what's going on outside of our walls should be prompting serious questions and transformation. Kerry Olitzky has the courage to ask those questions and the vision to shape new pathways for us all."
— Elyse D. Frishman, editor of *Mishkan T'filah* and senior rabbi of The Barnert Temple

"Rabbi Kerry Olitzky's case for "playlist Judaism" is a wake-up call for reality-based Jewish communal life, sensitive to today's most important cultural currents. Filled with accessible case studies and practical ideas for professionals and volunteers alike, it is an invaluable guidebook to a Jewish future that is already here."
— Shawn Landres, co-founder of Jewish Jumpstart, social entrepreneur, and writer

"*Playlist Judaism* provides us with both a still frame and a movie. It freezes this moment in time so that we can critically examine Jewish institutional strengths and limitations. But it moves from careful descriptions to

bold prescriptions—especially for synagogues. By offering analysis and direction, Olitzky enlarges our understanding of how synagogues can prepare and re-launch in this era of fundamental structural change."
— Hayim Herring, president, HayimHerring.com

"Kerry Olitzky has been helping the Jewish community better connect to all kinds of Jews for more than three decades. In *Playlist Judaism* he provides an invaluable manual of how Jewish organizations can do so much more effectively. If you care about engaging Next Gen Jews to Jewish life, make room on your shelf."
— Sid Schwarz, Senior Fellow, Clal: The National Jewish Center for Learning and Leadership and author, *Jewish Megatrends: Charting the Course of the American Jewish Community*

Playlist Judaism

Playlist Judaism

MAKING CHOICES FOR A VITAL FUTURE

KERRY M. OLITZKY

 ALBAN

Herndon, Virginia
www.alban.org

The Alban Institute
131 Elden St., Suite 202
Herndon, VA 20170

Bible translations from original Hebrew courtesy of the author.

Cover design by Daniel Belen, DBL Design Group.

Library of Congress Cataloging-in-Publication Data
    Olitzky, Kerry M.
    Playlist Judaism : making choices for a vital future / by Rabbi Kerry M. Olitzky.
        page cm
    Includes bibliographical references and index.
    ISBN 978-1-56699-439-2 (alk. paper)
    1. Judaism--United States. 2. Judaism--21st century. 3. Jews--United States--Identity. 4. United States--Religion. I. Title.
    BM205.O453 2013
    296.0973'09051--dc23
                                        2013016568

For Rabbi Avi S. Olitzky and Rabbi Jesse M. Olitzky, rabbis who will navigate the Jewish community of the future. May their torah be welcoming and their disciples numerous.

Contents

Foreword

I love music. I love to sing, especially during an ecstatic prayer experience or a good old-fashioned camp-like song session. I love to hear a great musician or symphony orchestra play music live—I have enjoyed wonderful summer evenings listening to the Los Angeles Philharmonic perform at the Hollywood Bowl. And, most recently, I plug into my iPhone, iPod, or iPad to access my personal playlist of favorite songs, downloaded from the millions of choices offered to me by iTunes.

This last opportunity to enjoy recorded music is a radically different alternative to my experience as a kid. In those days of yesteryear, there were two ways to buy tunes: a 45 rpm "single" record with two sides, A and B (A being the hit, B usually a less popular melody), or an LP (long-play) record album of some ten to twelve songs by one artist or band. The technology was a record player that used an arm with a diamond stylus that fit into the grooves of the vinyl disc, sending the signals through an amplifier and stereo speakers. This delivery system had a number of downsides. For example, there was always the risk of scratching the vinyl, which would mostly ruin the record, causing the stylus to skip or endlessly repeat sections of the track. But perhaps the most frustrating aspect of the experience was the necessity to endure those B-side tracks and the selection of mediocre songs that came as part of the album when it was really only one or two hits you wanted to hear.

Today, of course, there is no need to buy the whole album or put up with an inferior B side. Today, Internet-based technology enables me to choose only the songs I really want, the songs that really speak to me, the songs that make my own heart sing. Today, I create my personal playlist, my own mixtape of voices that move me.

In this perceptive and provocative book, Rabbi Kerry Olitzky brilliantly presents the notion of playlist as a metaphor for the limitless choices Jews and those living with Jews have today in shaping their personal experience of Judaism. The oft-cited aphorism "We are all Jews by choice" finds its ultimate expression in this twenty-first-century Playlist Judaism. The question is, What shall Jewish communal leaders, clergy, and educators do to engage a population that refuses to buy the whole album and increasingly picks only those experiences that resonate with who they are and where they are on their very personal spiritual journeys?

Earlier scholars have noted the fact that since arriving in large numbers with the waves of immigration at the beginning of the twentieth century, Jews quite quickly adopted the values of American individualism. The "you can't tell me how to live my life" attitude that permeates American culture inevitably creates a tension with a religious system that does dictate particular norms of behavior, standards of conduct, and a set of beliefs intended to shape a life of meaning and purpose. Arnold M. Eisen and Steven M. Cohen in their influential book *The Jew Within* called "the Jew within" a "sovereign self." These Jews make choices about how Jewish they will be yearly, monthly, even daily.

For synagogue leaders, this new reality is particularly challenging. Most of the several thousand congregations in North America continue to operate on the twentieth-century model of synagogue that evolved to meet the needs of a booming post–World War II Jewish community. Magnificent synagogue edifices were erected, more than a half million children (the baby boomers) populated their religious schools, and a steady stream of annual membership dues supported the hiring of full-time clergy, support staff, and teachers. Population surveys revealed that the vast majority of Jews joined a synagogue at one time or another during their adult years, often motivated by the desire to prepare their children for bar or bat mitzvah.

That was then; this is now. Late marriage has delayed the expected flow of members into congregations, while empty nesters who view the synagogue as mainly focused on families with children move to the periphery or out the door altogether. The result: the base of membership has narrowed significantly, threatening the financial stability of congregations. Consequently, many synagogues face downsizing, merging, or even going out of business.

Rabbi Olitzky, my colleague since his days as a key member of the Synagogue 2000 initiative founded by Rabbi Lawrence A. Hoffman and me in 1995, offers his own analysis of the current challenges facing synagogues, along with a number of bold predictions and solutions meant to chart a future path for synagogue leaders. As the driving force behind the Jewish Outreach Institute, Rabbi Olitzky has become one of the leading experts in guiding institutions interested in reaching the increasing numbers of unaffiliated Jews and those living with Jews. In what he notes are likely to be "controversial" ideas, he outlines ten key areas of work for those synagogues willing to take steps to transform themselves into spiritual communities that appeal to this elusive population.

I applaud Rabbi Olitzky for surfacing the challenges and charting a bold vision of how the leadership of the community might confront them. You may not agree with everything he proposes, but I assure you that the ideas and examples he cites will stimulate your thinking. Moreover, this book will provide synagogue leadership teams with a plethora of practical proposals to chart an exciting and engaging future for their congregations. I encourage you to study the book together and create your own playlist of strategies to adopt as you continue the critically important work of transforming your synagogue into a twenty-first-century sacred community.

Ron Wolfson

Fingerhut Professor of Education at American Jewish University, co-founder, Synagogue 3000/Next *Dor,* and author of *Relational Judaism: Using the Power of Relationships to Transform the Jewish Community*

Preface

I have been involved with synagogues my entire life, from the little Russian shul located in a neighbor's basement where my grandparents took me when I was a young child to the more modern suburban synagogues of later childhood and my adult life. I have also spent time praying in the various *shteibelach* (intimate prayer spaces) in Jerusalem as well as the great synagogues around the world. And I have searched out the forgotten synagogues nestled in small communities in the United States as well as the remnants of synagogues devastated by the Nazi war machine during World War II. My religious life has been nurtured by the synagogue, and I still use it as a lens through which to view Jewish religion. While I feel that many of my spiritual needs are met in the synagogue communities in which I actively participate, I constantly worry about their future.

In my tenure in the congregational rabbinate, right out of rabbinical school, I began my push for change in the synagogue. Then, while teaching at Hebrew Union College–Jewish Institute of Religion, the academic center and rabbinical school for the Reform Jewish movement, I continued to argue for significant change in the synagogue, particularly as a consultant for what is now Synagogue 3000, a transdenominational project to renew the synagogue primarily through the worship environment.

And now, as part of my work as executive director of the Jewish Outreach Institute (JOI), the only national, independent organization dedicated to reaching those who are unaffiliated, with a particular emphasis on the unaffiliated intermarried, I often work with synagogues that are grappling with their institutional viability. I stand as an insider, keenly aware of the perspective of the outsider. Because of my work, we at JOI have become the go-to resource on the Jewish future—futurists—especially since the implementation of the last JOI North American conference, Judaism2030. This conference boldly looked at the current trends and imagined what the Jewish community of the future might look like.

People are now aware of the urgent need to reimagine the synagogue if it is to survive, but they often do not understand the cultural trends that are currently affecting the synagogue and the entire Jewish community. Nor do they have the requisite skills to make necessary changes. This book provides the reader with an overview of the cultural context in which synagogues now find themselves and offers their leaders the insights and tools to make those changes, however difficult they may be.

I remain optimistic about the American Jewish future. Lots of important things are taking place in synagogues throughout North America. But they aren't being shared or promoted or celebrated. And the contemporary Jewish community cannot afford to rest on the success of previous generations if we want to guarantee the survival of the Jewish communal institutions in our midst, most notably the synagogue. Change will first require the hard, community soul wrenching that is outlined in these pages. Some of these pages may read like criticism of the synagogue and its leadership. Without the success of the past, however, we would not be in a position to make necessary changes. I see myself as a partner in the work of synagogue renewal, and I stand ready to help those who would like to put into action some of the suggestions set forth in these pages.

At the conclusion of each chapter, I have included several practical sections that will be of direct help to the reader. First, you will find things we know about the subject discussed in the chapter. This mostly takes the familiar form of a list of "ten things." Next comes a brief case study that reflects a successful implementation of the ideas suggested in the chapter. This is followed by a section called "Lessons Learned by . . . ," which emerges out of the case study. Finally, each chapter includes a few questions for synagogue leaders, so that they can begin to integrate the various ideas presented in the chapter and reflect on their potential impact in the synagogue.

Acknowledgments

I have shared these ideas with many people and in many places. While I could not begin to name all the people who might have reacted—positively and negatively—to the positions I have taken in these pages or the activities I have suggested, I do want to thank some individuals by name for making suggestions and discussing individual cases, sometimes about the institutions they lead: Rabbi Sharon Brous, Rabbi Jason Fruithandler, Rabbi Arnold Gluck, David Goodman, Rabbi Samuel Gordon, Stuart Himmelfarb, Rabbi Irwin Kula, Yehuda Kurtzer, Rabbi Naomi Levy, Rabbi Jeremy Morrison, Rabbi Scott Perlo, Rabbi Shira Stutman, Larry Weiss, and Ron Wolfson.

While the words in this volume are my own, I feel obliged to thank my staff colleagues and board members at Big Tent Judaism/Jewish Outreach Institute, the context in which many of these ideas were fleshed out and tested in the field. I am particularly grateful to Paul Golin, whose creative insights and sensitive wordsmithing are reflected in many of these pages. We at JOI are passionate about the work we do as we pave an optimistic path for the North American Jewish community to follow.

Words are inadequate to thank Beth Gaede, my editor. She worked with me each step along the way in developing this manuscript. While I take full responsibility for its contents, I could not have said what I wanted to say without her expert and supportive guidance. I also want to thank Andrea Lee, who copyedited the manuscript, and Lauren Belen at Alban, who shepherded this book from its inception to its completion. Finally, I thank my family for listening to me talk about these ideas over and over until I got them right. Sometimes the simplest words express the most profound sentiments. So I say a simple thank you to Sheryl, my life's partner, my soul mate, who constantly encourages me to think and act boldly, reassuring me that the work we do is for the sake of heaven.

Introduction

When historians write about the early twenty-first century in American Jewish history, they will most probably name it "the era of transition." We cannot be sure when this era will conclude. The only thing of which we can be sure is that the Jewish community will look nothing like it did when the era began. Every Jewish institution is undergoing significant change and is in danger of becoming irrelevant to the majority of North American Jews. All these institutions will have to reimagine themselves if they are to survive and grow. And the most numerous among these institutions is also the most vulnerable: the synagogue. The synagogue represents more investment in buildings and overhead than any other institution in the Jewish community, and its membership numbers are deteriorating the most rapidly. Its clergy are among the best compensated among religious institutions in North America, but people no longer see synagogue support as sufficiently important. This institution has served as the focal point of Jewish life and the center for worship for several generations in American Jewish life. If its continued existence is threatened, then perhaps the entire panoply of Jewish institutions is also at risk. I say this because, historically, lay leaders of other community institutions have come from the synagogue. Jewish communal service workers have been raised

1

in the synagogue. Jewish Federation financial supporters have been active synagogue members. This book explores the various megatrends and microtrends most affecting radical change in the Jewish communal enterprise and thereby having the most significant impact on the synagogue, its survival, and its growth.

A popularly held myth is that most North American Jewish institutions are ancient and have functioned in the same way for countless generations. While some institutions—like the cemetery, the synagogue, the school, and the home for the aged—date back to the beginnings of stationary Jewish neighborhood life, most are of relatively recent vintage. Each was introduced to serve a particular need, such as a place to bury the deceased, a place to pray, a center to educate children, and a facility to care for those elderly whose children were unable to care for them. Once those places were no longer needed the institution ceased to exist or at least became severely limited in its scope or influence—unless it evolved into a completely different institution. Consider the Jewish hospital, for example. The first Jewish hospital was established in Cincinnati, Ohio, in 1850. Responding to a cholera epidemic that devastated poor Jews in Cincinnati, the local community of Jews built this city's Jewish hospital—and others like it—to serve itinerant Jews (most often traveling peddlers) who were refused health care by other health care institutions, mostly those of particular religious denominations other than Judaism, of course. In addition, the Jewish hospitals provided a place for medical interns and residents to train at a time when they were not welcome at these other hospitals. These hospitals thrived for many decades, but as these particular needs for Jewish hospitals receded, so did the Jewish communal interest in supporting such generally mammoth institutions. Most of these hospitals have been sold and serve other functions.

The synagogue is now facing a similar challenge. Over the course of its development in North America, particularly during post–World War II suburbanization and baby boom, it took on a particular structure in response to a variety of needs—to educate children and to create an extended family when families moved out of the urban neighborhoods and into the suburbs, away from their families of origin. But needs of the Jewish people have changed. Most individuals no longer need the synagogue as a nexus for their social activities or as a primary location to network for professional advancement. And a variety of options are available for educating their children. Given this changing context, the purpose and function of the synagogue now must be reevaluated. There is a lot that Jewish leaders and any reader of this book don't know about the future and the needs of individuals, but there are many things we do know. For example, clergy and congregants know that the worship environment must engage the participant. Sacred drama in which the congregant sits passively in an audience doesn't work any longer, even if it once did. What is clear is that a different form of synagogue will emerge to serve the new needs of American Jewish religious life.

The contemporary needs of North American Jews are directly tied to the trajectory of the immigrant experience in North America. The generation now coming of age is the first generation we may call fully *American,* American Jews. While it may seem counterintuitive that immigration restrictions would enhance the American nature of the North American Jewish community, some scholars of American Jewish history will argue that the Jewish people became indigenous—and thereby fully American—in the United States as a result of the extremely restrictive Immigration Restriction Act of 1921 and the Immigration Act of 1924 (also called the Johnson-Reed Act). These acts of Congress limited immigration to the United States, which had been the primary source of Jewish expansion up until that time. The latter act superseded the Emergency Quota Act of 1921, which had been designed to aid the emigration of persecuted Jews from Poland and Russia, among other displaced populations. As a result of these limitations on immigration, the

Jewish people were no longer enriched by the Jewish cultures brought to the United States by immigrant Jews. Thus, the community began to develop its own identity as a North American Judaism and evolve on its own, becoming thoroughly American in the process. Nevertheless, the current generation of so-called millennials is the first in Jewish families never to have confronted the prejudice, limitations, and actual quotas faced by previous generations of American Jews. Consequently, this generation looks at Jewish communal institutions, particularly synagogues, differently from the way its parents or grandparents did. The synagogues make a different public statement for millennials than they did for their parents. For their parents, the synagogues represented a claim on American soil as citizens. For the millennials, the synagogues are just buildings that serve a Jewish communal and religious purpose. One might even go so far as to say there is nothing really sacred or special about synagogues for millennials—except for the religious functions they house. As a result, this generation is not prepared to support the edifices that the previous generation built or nurtured. Such institutions do not meet their needs or interests.

While the American synagogue was built with the financial support of what are commonly called three-day-a-year Jews, referring to those who may attend the synagogue for worship only on Rosh Hashanah and Yom Kippur, that generation of occasional synagogue attendees is losing interest in the synagogue. Thus, either people are fully embracing the synagogue—and willing to support and participate in it—or they are unwilling to support an institution in which they do not participate. Without support from these two groups, the synagogue may no longer be financially viable in its current form.

Yet, all is not lost. The experience of being fully American has also motivated large segments of millennials to embrace religious practices that their recent ancestors rejected out of fear, thinking that such practices would prevent them from becoming fully American. Consider the Reform movement in Judaism, for example. Its members are now embracing those very rituals and practices that the early Reformers rejected as too Jewish (read: not American enough). Ironically, the desire to become fully American was essentially what motivated the Reformers (in the United States) in the first place to shape Reform Judaism. Nothing can keep this generation from being fully American. At the same time, this notion of becoming fully American may account for the dramatic increase in intermarriage among millennials. Attitudes toward intermarriage have changed greatly as intermarried families have become more numerous. Synagogues have to grapple with the consequences and implications of this shift in attitude and population—a population that is at least half-intermarried. Thus, this book also identifies some of needs and interests of this generation in regard to its high rate of intermarriage and what the synagogue can do to meet those needs and address those interests. Other trends that have an impact on the synagogue will also be explored in this volume, including the entry of Judaism into the marketplace of ideas and the need to program for the largest population bubble in the North American community: the boomers.

Some will argue that the downturn in the economy—since 2008—has caused the synagogue to falter. I believe, however, that all the slowdown in the economy did was to force people to realize that these issues were bubbling under the surface of synagogue life. An expanding economy allowed leaders to ignore the problems. Those who still blame the woes of the synagogue on a faltering economy maintain that people are simply no longer able to afford the increasing costs of synagogue membership. Thus, the population base of the synagogue has shrunk. The same argument is being made by other Jewish institutions as well. In other words, all we have to do is fix the economic problems in the nation as a whole and the problems in the Jewish communal institutions will be resolved at the same time. But this is not the case. The challenge facing the synagogue is not an increase in the cost of membership. The challenge facing the synagogue is a decreasing cost benefit felt by its members.

While this book focuses on Jewish communal trends and their impact on the synagogue, the role of institutional leadership, particularly among clergy, must also be considered. Rabbi Irving ("Yitz") Greenberg, contemporary Orthodox theologian who founded Clal (The National Jewish Center for Learning and Leadership) and was president of the Jewish Life Network, argued thirty years ago that we were on the cusp of a change in leadership models that would drive the Jewish community into the future. Up until that time, and for the prior two thousand years, synagogue and communal authority rested primarily with the rabbi. While the term *rabbi* may still be used to refer to Jewish clergy, the role of such clergy, particularly as communal authority, has evolved considerably. I contend that as the synagogue further evolves, so must its religious leadership.

But this book is not just about academic theories. They alone are insufficient. Thus, this book also provides solutions to problems facing the synagogue that can be immediately applied, leading the reader to the ultimate goal of the book: to assist synagogue leaders in reshaping the synagogue so that it can reclaim its vital role in American Jewish religious life.

CHAPTER 1

Playlist Judaism

Napster, an Internet-based music file-sharing system that eventually lost its battle in the courts over copyrights and was forced to cease operations, helped change American culture. And in so doing, it unintentionally and unknowingly changed North American Jewish community culture as well, particularly for the synagogue. Consider what took place. Prior to the introduction of Napster, musicians and listeners depended on leaders of the music industry to determine whose music would be promoted and which songs would be made available to the public. These industry leaders determined release schedules and the prices of recorded music. They controlled almost every aspect of the industry. If musicians hoped to be heard beyond the local nightclub or café, they had to seek out a "label" to sponsor them. And the listener could purchase only what was made available through retail outlets. In an effort to break what many considered to be a stranglehold that music producers had on the music industry, Sean Parker, John Fanning, and Shawn Fanning, the founders of Napster, used Internet technology to shape a system that allowed people to seamlessly share music files with one another. Parker and the Fannings did so without any regard for copyright. Those who took advantage of what Napster had to offer did so without paying for this service and certainly without a fee to the musicians or their labels.

Napster stopped functioning, but it spawned hundreds of other systems that did similar kinds of things with other kinds of files, including Gnutella (a decentralized peer-to-peer network), Freenet (a peer-to-peer platform for censorship-resistant communication), Grokster (for sharing motion picture and music files), Madster (a file-sharing platform that uses instant messaging), and eDonkey (a network for sharing big files and for ensuring their long-term availability). Napster also opened up numerous possibilities for songwriters and musicians who were unable to get their music distributed through standard channels. It changed the entire music industry, which is still struggling for realignment. In the realm of music, the music industry lost its control over the personal listening habits of individuals. No longer would the individual have to purchase an entire album just to listen to one song (the only one perhaps that the listener really wanted to purchase in the first place). Moreover, with a little computer savvy, the individual could determine in what order he or she wanted to listen to music—and also could choose music directly from the musician without any intermediary. Napster and its successors on the Internet also gave the individual musician a vehicle to share his or her music directly with the consumer.

The music industry struggled—and continues to struggle— with this new normal. At first, in the midst of so much "free" music, the only companies making money on music were those whose songs were being used for ring tones on cellular telephones. Then Apple shaped an approach through the iTunes store that worked. They created a download system for individuals at a cost that seemed to be acceptable in the marketplace. The per-item profit that the iTunes store yielded was probably not what music companies were used to achieving, but it was a vast improvement over free downloading and a major step toward figuring out how to establish a business in the new market. But the real genius of Steve Jobs, head of Apple at the time, was the iPod, a device that could accommodate all these downloads, was portable, and was listener-centric. In other words, it was designed to accommodate the user rather than the music industry. What emerged from this was the personal *playlist*, a new cultural symbol. A playlist is a collection of songs that has been downloaded by the listener to a data-storing device that can be manipulated by the listener. Personal habits were inalterably changed as a result of the transformation of the music industry instigated by Napster and eventually evolving into the playlist.

Perhaps unbeknownst to the Jewish community, it too is feeling the impact of the changes brought on by Napster. This Internet-based customization set the tone for Jewish life as it did for American culture. Since the synagogue emerged on the scene in North America in the form we know it today, it has tried to control people's participation in various life-cycle and holiday events to protect its financial membership base. Synagogue leaders did not trust their members to pay their membership dues without such persuasion. If you wanted your child to mark a bar or bat mitzvah at the synagogue, you had to be a member of that synagogue with your financial obligations up-to-date. If you wanted tickets for High Holiday services (the only way you were permitted entry in most synagogues), then you had to be a member of that synagogue, paid in full. If you appeared at some synagogues for the High Holidays and you were not current, then someone might usher you into the "membership office" to straighten out your account. It was a closed system with little or no opportunity to participate in it any other way.

Some independent rabbis provided bar or bat mitzvah education and ceremonies outside the synagogue. Similarly, some institutions provided High Holiday tickets either free or without the need to pay dues to that synagogue. Most of these approaches were limited in their success and in their duration.

These alternatives to the practices of established synagogue institutions were generally not taken seriously by the organized Jewish community, however. Often they were disregarded as the work of unsanctioned fringe groups. On occasion they were intentionally undermined by a cabal formed by local rabbinic groups or synagogue councils, along with Jewish communal institutions supported by the local Jewish Federation, to prevent them from destabilizing the status quo.

Under the influence of the cultural change instigated by Napster, those in the North American Jewish community borrowed the American icon created by Apple and the iPod and began following what I like to call Playlist Judaism. No longer did they want anyone else to determine how they might "Jew it." And they certainly didn't want to pay for membership just so that they could have High Holiday tickets or celebrate the bar or bat mitzvah of their child. They wanted to pick and choose the Judaism that worked for them and to pay only for the synagogues services they desired. At the same time, the so-called destination bar or bat mitzvah was appearing on the scene, as were free High Holiday services, pioneered by Chabad but not limited to one particular Jewish religious group. In other words, bar or bat mitzvahs began to take place outside synagogues—without the services or control of a rabbi and without the cost of synagogue dues. American Jews reasoned that the playlist approach worked in other parts of their lives. Why wouldn't the playlist model work Jewishly as well? But synagogues have not been responsive to such an approach, and so members—even longstanding members— have been walking away from them. Only now as membership plunges—expedited but not caused by economic decline—are synagogues beginning to rethink the implications of Playlist Judaism and how they can respond to them.

The local synagogue is not alone in its struggle over the decentralization of American culture in general and Playlist Judaism in particular. For example, most synagogues are affiliated with a particular Jewish religious movement. Similar to the way the synagogue is affected on the local level, the religious movements are affected on the national level by Playlist Judaism. And the national movements are attempting to respond by tightening their control of rabbinic placement, something they have done with relative success for several generations. Synagogues can't pick and choose what services they want their national body to provide. If they want the opportunity to select movement-trained rabbis and cantors to serve them, then the synagogues have to pay dues to the national body. So some synagogues—to ensure the widest pool of rabbinic candidates and to avoid paying dues for movement services they are not interested in—are seeking clergy outside the movement-sponsored training institutions.

The local synagogue is asking the national Jewish religious movement with which it is affiliated the same question members are asking their own synagogue. How is the national movement serving us, the local synagogue? What is the benefit of the fees we pay to the national movement? And so the synagogue may be seen severing its ties with the national movement for the same reason that individuals may decide that affiliation with the synagogue is not worth it for them. The same kind of challenge is being faced by other Jewish communal institutions affiliated with national organizations. These national organizations have no control over their constituents. Like the synagogue and its members, they enter into a voluntary covenant with one another. Each member is able to discontinue his or her relationship at will—and does so with little remorse or regret.

People who might have once been synagogue members are now looking for an episodic connection to institutions. There is no longer any concern for "stickiness" or what might be described as a longer-lasting connection. This lack of association with institutions is evident throughout North American culture. Consider the Steppenwolf Theatre in Chicago, for example. After years of robust subscription sales, its sales started slipping. When it studied its decrease in subscription sales and a simultaneous increase in individual ticket sales, the theater company also realized that its practice of privileging its subscribers over those who were purchasing single tickets had been based on a mistaken assumption: that single-ticket purchasers didn't want more out of the theater experience. The company learned, however, that these single-ticket theatergoers did not want *less* of a relationship with the theater. Rather, they simply wanted a *different* relationship. Just like the synagogue member, they were not passing up season tickets (or full synagogue membership) because they didn't want *any* relationship. They wanted to change the terms of the relationship and still be served.

Membership in the synagogue has been determined by paying membership dues. And the presumption has been that these members form a community. In some cases, dues-paying members really feel that they are part of a synagogue. In most cases, community membership is a bit of a contrived notion, since it is based only on paying dues, not on participation in the life of the synagogue. When synagogues were neighborhood institutions, they actually served the local neighborhood. Once people started to leave Jewish enclaves and drive to the synagogues, the idea that membership and community were related was no longer true. As a result, community itself has become a difficult idea to describe and access. *Community* has simply become a euphemism for paying dues, and then members have been assessed fees for particular services on top of their dues. These fees have really become surcharges levied on the members over and above the costs of individual dues. Here is how it has worked: since the individual is not able to celebrate the bar or bat mitzvah of a child without paying for synagogue membership, the individual is forced to pay membership dues (usually for a minimum number of years). Those dues entitle that person to pay additional fees for the cost of tutoring the child, among other costs. This fee system makes it quite clear to the member that paying membership dues is more about financing the synagogue than participating in a group.

Before we consider alternatives to membership, it is important to understand the attitude and culture created by an emphasis on membership. Affiliation—primarily based on payment of dues to the synagogue—becomes the driving force for the synagogue to reach out to newcomers (anyone who is not a member). This drive to recruit dues-paying members emerges in the language that describes lay leadership (membership chairperson, membership committee) as well as the professional leadership of the congregation (membership director). And as soon as newcomers appear on the scene, they are solicited for membership. All these efforts are made because synagogue leaders think that membership dues are the only path to financial stability. And as the financial health of a synagogue declines, the stress on approaching potential members—who will by definition pay dues—intensifies. Those responsible for the well-being of the synagogue presume that once they get newcomers to affiliate, they will become engaged by the institution and what it has to offer. And they are not really willing to engage individuals (or permit access to most synagogue services, especially the significant ones) until they are affiliated (as dues-paying members).

I argue that synagogue leaders have it backwards. Engaging individuals is what will lead them to affiliate with a synagogue as the institution that serves them, that meets their needs and those of their family. If synagogues continue to focus on the needs of the institution rather than on the needs of the individual, they will lose their dues-paying members and eventually become financially unviable. Rabbi Abraham Joshua Heschel suggested to folks in the 1960s that they pray with their feet—and those prayers took them to places like the civil rights marches in Selma, Alabama. As a result of the actions of Rabbi Heschel and the influence of American political culture, American Jews—like most Americans—have been taught to vote with their feet. And that vote may help them march away from the synagogue if the synagogue doesn't find effective ways to engage them.

Ironically, it was the liberal American synagogue that introduced membership dues to the religious community. The dues system was considered to be a novel approach to the finances of a religious institution, a better system than churches' practice of collecting tithes or passing the weekly collection plate. It was considered better because it was more dependable. Leaders could better project their finances, the funds that would be available to them to engage clergy and pay for services as well as cover the general overhead associated with the physical plant. Synagogue leaders thought people would feel ownership of an institution they supported as dues-paying members. But now, with the culture of choice firmly established, the very system that helped them grow is failing them.

Alternatives to the Membership Model

Some institutions will want to cling to the membership model, arguing that the maintenance of the membership model is an example of the countercultural approach that Jewish life has always taken. "It's OK," so they say, "that others are abandoning this model. We believe in community, and dues-paying membership is the only way to maintain it." And so they simply hang on, thinking that some institutions using the standard dues-paying membership model will survive. They think that this is the historical model and that tradition alone is sufficient reason to maintain it. They also reason that some segments of the synagogue will not want any changes in the structure of membership or the relationship of members to the synagogue as described above and will want to maintain the synagogue as they have known it. They are probably correct. But too many synagogue leaders delude themselves into believing that their institution will be the one to survive intact and that if these *other* institutions want to survive, *they* are the ones that will have to approach the membership model anew.

Synagogues don't have to cling to the model they think is the only option available to them. There are alternatives. Some synagogues are simply calling themselves *community institutions* rather than *membership institutions* that require payment of dues to become a member. These synagogues suggest that all locals are members of the synagogue and therefore welcome to use its services or the services of its professional staff. Like online services that are free, these congregations would charge only for upgrades or premium services, such as personal or family counseling by the rabbi or the education of children.

Some institutions are opting for totally voluntary dues. In this case, they are not suggesting any specific fee and counting on the generosity of people in their orbit. With experiments from High Holiday ticket sales, they have learned that they are actually able to raise more funds without specifying an amount and opening their doors wider to what might be called Big Tent Judaism. Some of these institutions are taking their annual expenses and dividing them by the number of what they consider to be membership units. This determines a per-membership unit cost that they share with the membership as a benchmark of sorts. Temple Israel, a large suburban congregation in Sharon, Massachusetts, took this approach in 2008. Each time they raised dues, their numbers declined. So they opted for a voluntary approach. While revenue declined the first two years of the new policy, revenue increased beginning the third year. And the new policy attracted twenty new families that same year. According to its leaders, the increase in membership cannot be directly attributed to the change in dues policy, but they believe the new practice contributed to the growth.

Others are advocating specialized memberships, such as a High Holiday membership or a bar or bat mitzvah family membership. In this way, people have to pay only for the level of services that they are intending to use at the synagogue. Irrespective of their level of service, they become members of the synagogue.

Still others are looking toward a fee-for-service model, one in which people pay only for the services they use and treat the synagogue professionals as they would any other professional in the community—such as physicians, lawyers, and accountants—and pay them accordingly. There is no membership at all. Perhaps the folks who do not maintain the traditional member relationship with the synagogue might better be called clients. While the fee-for-service model will work for education and life-cycle events, it is not yet clear whether people will be willing to pay professional fees to clergy members for counseling or guidance, for example. And how would synagogues assess fees for prayer services—which have ostensibly always been free—outside of the High Holidays, a practice for which there is no precedent at all?

TEN PRINCIPLES OF PLAYLIST JUDAISM

1. People want to control their own religious life.
2. The center of their Jewish life is built around them, as individuals, rather than around an institution, especially a singular one.
3. There is no intrinsic value in membership.
4. People want to shape their own participation in religious life.
5. People want their Jewish life to be voluntary rather than obligatory.
6. Free does not imply that the object or service that is free has no value or investment. Instead, free access is a positive value.
7. People want to choose (and pay for) only those things that speak to them.

8. People do not want the things that meet their needs bundled with other things that they don't think meet their needs and thereby be forced to buy the entire package.
9. Synagogues have to be flexible enough to welcome such personal choices and offer individuals a panoply of options to engage Jewish life.
10. Options for participation must emerge from the interest of individuals rather than the needs of the synagogue so that individuals can freely create their own Playlist Judaism.

Sixth and I Historic Synagogue

Sixth and I Historic Synagogue (named for the cross-streets where the synagogue is located) in Washington DC provides us with a working example of Playlist Judaism. There are no membership fees, and people who participate in its programs pay for those individual programs. The synagogue was dedicated in 1908 to be the home of Adas Israel, a Conservative synagogue established as an alternative to the district's first Jewish house of worship, a Reform synagogue: Washington Hebrew Congregation. Both congregations still function in the district and are major Jewish communal institutions. The original Adas Israel building was sold in 1951 to Turner Memorial AME Church, and Adas Israel relocated to Connecticut Avenue and Quebec Street. When Turner Memorial congregants moved into their new sanctuary in Maryland in 2002, following the outmigration of members to the suburbs, the former synagogue was put up for sale. The building was purchased by three local philanthropists (Washington Wizards owner Abe Pollin and local real-estate developers Shelton Zuckerman and Douglas Jemal) who were committed to returning the building to undefined Jewish communal use and rededicated it in 2004 following its extensive refurbishment. Not surprisingly, in the incipient stages the effort met with resistance from the organized Jewish community—and now the community champions its work as Sixth and I successfully reaches the elusive twenties and thirties population.

Following some false starts to define its mission and program (and the relatively short tenures of two executive directors), the synagogue, sees itself, in its own words, "as a place where people, especially those in their twenties and thirties, can connect to Judaism, arts, and culture both religiously and socially. At Sixth and I what it means to be Jewish is up to *you*. With a multidenominational and nonmembership approach, it is an ongoing experiment in creating a uniquely Jewish experience, where identity and community intersect on *your* terms. Sixth & I introduces young professionals and Jews of all ages to an unconventional, inclusive model of twenty-first-century Jewish life."

The background of its current executive director, Esther Safran Foer, is in public relations. She employed that background (and her contacts) to mold Sixth and I into a sought-after venue for the arts, with an astounding array of authors and speakers. It was also under her direction that Sixth and I discontinued any family or children's programming as well as any programming for adults in age segments other than the twenties and thirties.

Among its creative approaches to Jewish life was the establishment of the Sixth and Rye kosher food truck. While it had a limited life, the truck was parked in a variety of settings on Fridays, in anticipation of Shabbat (the Sabbath). Even those who may not be traditionally observant enjoyed purchased *challot* (braided egg bread for the Sabbath). It is not clear why it ceased operation and why Sixth and I didn't encourage its return. Nevertheless, this was another example of creatively going where people are.

The synagogue originally saw itself as simply a place where multiple minyanim (prayer groups), formed by any Jews in the community, could meet. When Rabbi Shira Stutman, a graduate of the Reconstructionist Rabbinical College, was added to the staff, she sought to bring what she called "quality control" to the worship service experience. Sixth and I had developed a "brand strategy," and the leadership at the synagogue wanted to make sure that every worship experience reflected the integrity of that brand. As a result, Sixth and I discontinued the practice of making its space available to other rabbis and independent prayer groups and instead built its own services and programs, which quickly became filled to capacity.

Sixth and I invited Rabbi Scott Perlow to join its staff and build on Stutman's work. He shaped a prayer life for Sixth and I participants and built community among its target population. The approach undertaken by Stutman and Perlow required them to transcend the episodic connection people had with Sixth and I. Neither Stutman nor Perlow were interested in building an alternative to mainstream synagogues. They committed themselves to serving only a specific population, and they know that this population is transitory but is not prepared to age along with them. So they built bridges to more traditional institutions in the Jewish community, particularly local synagogues. By doing so, they see themselves adding to the population of change agents in these local institutions or, at the very least, nurturing allies for change—since they recognize that the local community synagogues may not be able to provide continuity for the worship experiences provided by Sixth and I.

Lessons Learned by Sixth and I

1. Establishing a partnership with local synagogues is important if these institutions are going to be prepared to welcome those who have been reached by an alternative institution.
2. Narrowing the focus to a particular target population may mean that the community is unstable, because participants will age in and out.

3. Quality control of programs is important to the branding of an institution.
4. To succeed in a climate of change in the Jewish community, institutions have to be nimble.
5. It is just as important to establish groups of followers who are seeking change as it is to foster leaders who will be instrumental in making change.

Reflection and Discussion Questions for Synagogue Leaders

1. How do you help large numbers of people navigate their journey from one institution to another and still keep that journey intimate and personal?
2. In what ways can a synagogue strive to serve distinct target populations even if those populations are transitory?
3. To what extent is the spiritual environment of an institution shaped by the individual personalities or interests of its spiritual leaders? What are the advantages and disadvantages of building a spiritual environment according to the inclination of institutional leaders?

Sixth and I has established a successful model for reaching the elusive twenty- and thirtysomethings. If other institutions follow their lead, they will be able to reach that population as well. Moreover, if they join with alternative institutions to build bridges in the community from one institution to another, the entire community will be strengthened.

CHAPTER 2

Turning the Synagogue Inside Out

Since its inception, the synagogue in North America has focused primarily on providing services to its members in its facility. In particular, the attention of the clergy to family life-cycle events has been considered one of the many benefits of membership in the synagogue. Moreover, congregants have been supported by the congregation during other liminal moments in their lives. As members, congregants have had direct access to all that the synagogue had to offer. They have owned a share of the enterprise, so they have voted—or, at least, have had the right to vote—on any synagogue issue of concern to them.

While the term *member* is still used today by most synagogues, the relationship of the so-called member to the synagogue has been altered. This evolution occurred imperceptibly over time. Yet, only recently have synagogue leaders begun to discern that a problem with membership may be lurking, one that is more serious than just member attrition rates. While the dues model for synagogue membership has to change (as presented in chapter 1), the synagogue also needs to significantly change its model of program and service delivery.

To emphasize what is required for this proposed change—which is quite substantial—I like to say that I believe the synagogue needs to *turn itself inside out*. In other words, it has to become an institution that serves the entire local Jewish community—and, in some cases, secularists too—rather than functioning solely as an institution that serves only its members. When synagogues turn themselves inside out, all Jews and all those in Jewish families in the local area become members of the synagogue simply by virtue of their living in the synagogue's newly defined service area. They are then entitled to the membership benefits of the institution. (Premium membership could perhaps be available at an extra charge.) Moreover, the synagogue has to be willing to program beyond its walls, in public spaces. This is what I call Public Space Judaism.

We talk about the Jewish community—the synagogue community—as if we are talking about its majority, or even the whole. However, when we use the term *Jewish community*, we are generally speaking about only a minority of Jews in a region—those who are members of synagogues or Jewish Community Centers or those who support the local Jewish Federation financially with a campaign gift. In reality, the majority are not affiliated with these three institutions and do not financially support them.

Turning the synagogue inside out is a method to serve the majority of the Jewish community, even its entirety, rather than just those who are members of Jewish institutions. This notion will undoubtedly provoke a barrage of criticism from institutional leaders and members. After all, how can an institution serve an entire area when it doesn't have the sufficient resources to serve its institutional members? The clergy and other professional staff members are stretched to capacity. They can't do any more. Besides, why should people who do not pay dues to a synagogue (understood as those who are not paying for the services provided by the synagogue) be entitled to the services that are indeed provided by that synagogue for its dues-paying members? And how can such an approach be undertaken at a time when the synagogue is losing financial support as a result of diminishing membership? In any case, how does the synagogue determine how far it can extend its geographic reach into the surrounding neighborhoods and beyond if not by where its members live? Finally, why would the synagogue invest in a magnificent—often architecturally significant—building only to program outside the building?

These are all legitimate questions and concerns. However, I believe that the change proposed in this chapter is a necessary response to these challenges—already stretched financial and human resources and continuously dwindling membership and support—and should not be limited by them. This change addresses the needs of the upcoming generation, whose view of the synagogue is quite different from their parents' view. It will also help the synagogue reach people where they are, rather than forcing people to cross its threshold for service. Further, because the parents of this upcoming generation are often taking their cues from their children, this new model will appeal to them. The appeal to the parents—the so-called boomers—will be addressed more extensively in chapter 5.

Changing Views of the Synagogue

Jews in North America established congregations and built synagogues for numerous reasons. The very presence of a local synagogue made an important statement on behalf of the Jews who lived in that locality, most of whom were either immigrants or the children of immigrants. Rather than struggling with the limitations forced on their predecessors in Europe (whose synagogues could not be located on a major thoroughfare or facing the street in most of Hungary, and could not be as tall as neighboring churches in villages in Poland, for example), American synagogues could be built anywhere, in any shape or size. The American synagogue was a sign to others that Jews lived in the midst of or alongside all other religious and ethnic communities. That synagogues were granted the same status as churches meant that Jews were American citizens, equal to their non-Jewish neighbors and with full rights.

The history of North American Jews not only made them proud and grateful to construct synagogues in their new communities. It also led them to conduct programs inside their synagogues, because their experiences in other countries made them wary of being visible. But established in a safe environment, the North American synagogue served a variety of purposes for at least 150 years. Contemporary rabbis like to say—borrowing from their rabbinic predecessors—that the synagogue functioned as a house of prayer (*bet tefillah*), a house of study (*bet midrash*), and a place of assembly (*bet knesset*). Within the walls of these synagogues, there was a place to pray, a place to educate Jewish children (usually in a supplementary school rather than a day school), and a place to socialize with neighbors and make new friends. However, the synagogue was a house of prayer only for the small minority who came to its regular worship services (except for the High Holidays, when the largest number of Jews made their way to the synagogue). It was a house of study primarily for the children of members and the few adults who chose to attend a lecture or take a course. And it became a place to assemble the community only on rare occasions, such as when an emergency confronted the state of Israel, and for those invited to life-cycle events, such as a wedding or a bar or bat mitzvah. The synagogue also became a place for networking, as professionals sought out new clients and businesses sought out new customers. Moreover, these synagogues provided a sacred place for burying the deceased—since the synagogue was often affiliated with or owned a cemetery. Other life-cycle events could also be celebrated or marked there.

Members of the millennial generation neither view the synagogue building as necessary proof that Judaism is a fully accepted member of North America's faith life nor feel the need to express their Jewish identity only behind the closed doors of synagogue and home. The millennial generation has grown up in an era when the existence of the state of Israel is taken for granted, and the nation is viewed as a powerful military force and friend of the United States. The Holocaust, which destroyed six million Jews, might as well be ancient history to this generation of privilege. This is also a time in U.S. history when blatant anti-Jewish incidents are relatively few and insignificant. As the synagogue eventually took its place firmly among other houses of worship in North America, the contemporary synagogue took cues about its function from these other institutions much more than it did from other synagogue models in Jewish history. In a sense, the American synagogue became for Jews in North America what the church had become for Christians in North America. Slowly the synagogue gave away its study and assembly functions to other Jewish institutions that grew up around it. Day schools and other educational institutions became the houses of study. The Jewish Community Center (JCC) became the place of assembly. It is important to note that many of these institutions have diminished in size, drastically changed their raison d'etre, or ceased to exist entirely. So worship has become the function around which the synagogue currently functions. It is ironic, therefore, that few attend its worship services.

Synagogue leaders have yet to realize that the synagogue has once again become essentially a house of prayer. Many of the alternative synagogue structures that are emerging—primarily led by young people—are built solely around prayer services. Instead of accepting this default position, synagogues need to take what they do best—if they can indeed do them better than any other institution in the Jewish landscape—and locate their "brand" in the broader community. Synagogues need to be open to those issues that are engaging people in contexts outside the synagogues. For example, there is a growing interest in food justice issues, particularly among millennials, yet few synagogues have built their programs around this issue.

As mentioned in the introduction to this volume, synagogues, as well as other institutions in the Jewish community, were built on the foundation of what are somewhat pejoratively called three-day-a-year Jews, those who attend worship services at the synagogue only on the High Holidays. Since World War II, this population—while still a minority of American Jews yet a majority of synagogue members—has financially supported synagogues (and other Jewish communal institutions) by paying membership dues even if they didn't participate. Ari Kelman, a research sociologist, has argued that synagogues would be incapable of serving their members if all their members actually participated regularly in the synagogue, even though that is considered the ideal vision of synagogue leaders. Kelman argues that because the system in which those who pay dues do not participate remains capable of providing the foundation for Jewish institutions, the community should allow the system to continue. However, these three-day-a-year Jews are disappearing from our dues-paying membership ranks. Fewer and fewer Jews are willing to support an institution in which they do not participate, and they are not interested in attending even High Holiday services in the large numbers they once did. Instead, they will only support those institutions in which they regularly participate.

Barriers to Participation

It is important to identify those elements that might cause individuals to distance themselves from the synagogue in the first place. The synagogue is a high-barrier institution. As it currently stands, people have to make a significant effort to step over the threshold of a synagogue. The first barrier is what I call the location barrier. The location where an event or program is held can be a deterrent to participation, although people familiar with the venue may take for granted the location of a program (especially in a synagogue or other Jewish communal institution). But it might not be in a convenient location for the potential participant. There are other barriers too. Possibly the synagogue conjures up unpleasant childhood memories that cause the potential participant discomfort upon entering and, as a result, he or she does not do so. Of course, such memories are not necessarily restricted to childhood. Potential program participants may hold memories of other unpleasant synagogue encounters. Or perhaps the behavioral expectations, what psychologists call scripts, are unknown to the potential participant. So rather than being placed in a situation where she or he does not know what is expected, that person forgoes participation. The threshold for entry is just too high to traverse. Some may call these cultural obstacles, which include a lack of Jewish literacy or familiarity with the Jewish culture code expected of program participants. Cost is a significant barrier for many, as is scheduling (the timing of the program). For those who are intermarried, or perhaps members of a subgroup who has been historically sidelined or disenfranchised by the synagogue, they may simply feel unwelcome. That too is a barrier for entry.

Public Space Judaism

Public Space Judaism is designed to address these barriers. The notion emerges from the foundational idea of *outreach*, as I understand it. Outreach is not about a specific target population. Rather, it is a methodology. Outreach methodology brings Jewish life to a variety of traditionally underserved populations by going where people areinstead of waiting for them to come to us.

Where most Jews are *not* is inside the four walls of synagogues. We know that free or low-cost Jewish programs held in secular venues attract less-affiliated participants than the same programs held in synagogues or JCCs. Why not program where people spend the majority of time—outside in public spaces—rather than inside the synagogue, where most programs currently take place?

The location barrier is arguably the most important, because even if all other barriers have been lowered, those folks who have felt pushed away in the past are too hesitant to enter synagogues to see what's changed. While the Public Space Judaism model is based on location, it also addresses several additional barriers to participation and takes into consideration the necessary best practices of outreach, which include the unobtrusive collection of contact information and a specific follow-up plan. The goal is not to water down Judaism but to remove the cultural obstacles that have developed around Judaism—obstacles that may have had a purpose at one time but now push more people away than they keep in. Public Space Judaism is a portal of entry. It is not an immersive Jewish experience.

The Public Space Judaism model can be described as a series of concentric circles. The circle in the center reflects deeper institutional involvement, while the nonparticipating majority of Jewish households are in the outermost circle. The outermost ring gives this model its name and consists of events and programs that take place in public spaces. These events are designed so that potential participants "stumble over" them. They are low barrier in that they are free and require no prior knowledge or commitment to participate. Chabad pioneered this notion of outreach thirty years ago, and while my approach—championed by the Jewish Outreach Institute—in these spaces differs considerably, there is much to learn from Chabad's successes. Chabad is focused on the Jewish calendar, for example, but people live within a framework of several calendars, including but not limited to the Jewish calendar, the secular calendar, and the local cultural calendar. Public Space Judaism takes advantage of the various calendars that guide people's lives. It also insinuates itself into public events already taking place in the community.

The second level of Public Space Judaism is what I call Destination Jewish Culture. These programs are also low barrier and held in secular spaces. However, they usually require some level of planned participation (a set start time and destination event) and may charge a nominal fee (though no more than what would be charged at a secular equivalent). Good examples of programs that might fit in this circle are Jewish film festivals held in commercial theaters or a Jewish musical event held in a concert hall.

The third level of Public Space Judaism is what might be described as Open Door Community programs. These may be held within Jewish communal institutions, but they are open to the entire community. A good example of this approach is the Reform Jewish movement's Taste of Judaism program (although the program is not limited to the Reform movement). This brief three-week introduction to Judaism is free, welcomes all participants regardless of background, and is geared specifically for adult beginner learners. Also, the program is advertised in secular media.

Some people are critical of Public Space Judaism. It is important to note that I am advocating holding events in the public sphere (or spaces), not in the so-called public square, in order to avoid what some people think of as traversing the separation of church and state. Nonetheless, there are those who fear a slippery slope from public spaces to the public square. They also misunderstand Public Space Judaism as a form of missionary activity. Its intent is not to encourage people to convert to Judaism. Rather, it is designed to bring Judaism out to where people are. It is not intended to be "in your face." Finally, some believe that Judaism should not be "out there," since they are fearful of any anti-Jewish sentiment that it might stir up. A well-executed Public Space Judaism program responds to these concerns in effective implementation.

If we turn the synagogue inside out, the synagogue would serve a far broader audience, one that is not restricted by the traditional notion of synagogue membership. Synagogues can reach out and serve a population larger than their current membership if they are willing to emphasize those things that the synagogue does well and that are within its purview, while refraining from those things that are irrelevant to the synagogue and its work. In too many situations, synagogue professional staff members are stretched to capacity because they are asked to do things that are of no direct benefit to the individuals they serve. Often, their time is consumed by endless meetings, many of which do not relate to their work or to representing the synagogue in public events. In an inside-out synagogue, clergy will have time to serve the greater community if the synagogue, particularly its lay board of directors, refrains from requiring its clergy to take upon themselves work that is better accomplished by others, such as fund-raising and administrative tasks. In addition, once the synagogue becomes a community institution, anyone touched by the synagogue will have reason to provide for its financial well-being. Since the catchment area of synagogues is not always self-evident, this model allows for the synagogue's leadership to determine its logical geographic reach and demographic target populations.

While the notion is undoubtedly controversial, I argue that when a synagogue turns itself inside out, it can provide for life-cycle events and education for everyone without making a distinction as to who is a member and who is a nonmember. This also allows the synagogue to reclaim the functions that it gave away to day schools, JCCs, and others. In reality, four life-cycle events have theoretically been under the hegemony of the modern synagogue. These are the events that surround birth, coming of age, marriage (including divorce), and death. Many synagogues will name babies for parents who are not members, presuming that one day they might become members. And more often than not, those who marry are not synagogue members, since they no longer live in their hometowns and, as young singles, have not been motivated to join a synagogue in their new city of residence. Following the common trajectory of synagogue membership, by the time people die (in old age), they have already discontinued their synagogue membership, although perhaps their children are still members. Thus, some synagogues do funerals for people who are technically not members. In practice, the synagogue generally limits its services only to members in the area of bat or bar mitzvah. Most life-cycle events (outside of these four core events) that individuals mark, such as getting a drivers license or graduating from college, are outside the purview of the synagogue. And for life-cycle events that used to be a benefit of synagogue membership, such as bar or bat mitzvahs and weddings, families are looking outside of the synagogue for assistance. This new model allows the synagogue to reach a larger target population and expand its ability to bring Judaism together with important milestones, beyond the traditional four, in a person's life.

Turning the synagogue inside out, into a community institution, means that it has to become a recognizable presence. The building used to be the vehicle to make its presence known. Now the building is taken for granted, even if people are able to discern what takes place inside it. This model depends on a different approach. By turning inside out, the synagogue will make its presence known in two ways: by implementing Public Space Judaism programs in various locations throughout the year and by branding its work.

The overall program model could provide a route for the individual into deeper engagement with the synagogue. An unaffiliated newcomer happens upon some Public Space Judaism event that she will enjoy participating in and begins to feel more comfortable at Jewish events. While there, she will also learn of an upcoming Destination Jewish Culture event that interests her. Attending destination events increases her interest and alerts her to an Open Door Community event. Attending that event in turn excites her about that program's host synagogue. That then takes her to core Jewish communal programs inside the synagogue.

Through this idealized sequence of what can be called next steps, newcomers are provided with fun, meaningful, multiple Jewish contacts and gradually feel drawn deeper into Jewish communal life. In reality, the journey is much more complex. All stages can serve as entry points, and the progression is not necessarily the shortest distance between two points. Some folks may participate in public space events for years, but if they had previously been doing nothing Jewish, this represents successful outreach, because the goal is increasing engagement. They will go deeper when specific programs of greater complexity are relevant for them. Increasing engagement is not a membership drive. It is sharing what we inside the synagogue find beautiful about Judaism with others who might benefit from it.

How to Implement Public Space Judaism in Ten Steps

1. Go where people are. Don't wait for them to come to you. Hold events in the public sphere so that the unaffiliated will stumble upon them.

2. Start with a program or event that may be familiar to potential participants, such as Passover or Hanukkah. Charge no entry fee to keep the barriers low for participation.

3. As an option, take an event or program already planned and move it into a public space. Or take a longer multisession program and divide it into individual stand-alone events. Also, plan events as part of the secular community-at-large calendar, such as local fairs and parades.

4. Always design events to appeal to a defined target audience. Focus on the needs of the potential participant, not the needs or interests of the sponsoring institution.

5. Make sure the event is convenient for potential participants to attend. Identify arts, music, and cultural venues
   that your target audience frequents, including bookstores,
   theaters, concert halls, and athletic centers.
6. Market your programs in secular venues and through
   secular media outlets.
7. Recruit and train a sufficient number of staff and volunteers for the event to help make personal connections with
   participants and learn of their needs and interests.
8. Collaborate with other institutions in the community to
   develop a more effective program. This also allows you to
   extend the geographic reach of the program and multiply
   the number of events you can sponsor.
9. Invite participants to follow-up events that are consistent
   with their needs and interests and with the event they
   are attending. The path to deeper engagement requires a
   charted course.
10. You never get a second chance to make a first impression.
    Make sure that the event is appealing. Moreover, every
    experience, even introductory ones such as Public Space
    Judaism events, should have value and meaning.

The Riverway Project

The Riverway Project at Temple Israel in Boston was concep-
tualized by Rabbi Jeremy Morrison. As someone who grew up
in Boston and attended the synagogue there, he understood
the synagogue's strengths and the challenges it faced. Thus, he
proposed opening a storefront presence for the synagogue in
Boston's South End, a neighborhood in the process of gentrifica-
tion and where many of the synagogue's elusive target population of twenty- and thirty-year-olds live. The project was named

for the location of the current Temple Israel, yet the Riverway Project took place in the general neighborhood where Temple Israel had occupied its first sanctuary—and had vacated as the Jewish population moved.

Early on Morrison realized that occupying an actual space would be an obstacle to encouraging people to participate in programs and worship experiences. It is also true that the leaders of the sponsoring institution, Temple Israel, feared the financial implications for the synagogue. Moving from "places to people," as Morrison named this approach, he began to have house meetings with his intended population of twenty- and thirtysomethings, trying to engage them and, at the same time, gauge their interest in connecting with the organized Jewish community.

So in 2001, abandoning the idea of a storefront operation, Morrison and his wife rented an apartment, and their living room became the locus for his work and a gathering place for those whom he was trying to reach. As part of the project, he also gathered people in other neighborhoods, using an apartment that a local "connector" rented or owned in another neighborhood. According to Morrison:

> Riverway events that occur outside of Temple Israel's building but happen in participants' neighborhoods and living-rooms are considered an "extension" of Temple Israel, and all of our programming is conducted at times and in places that are conducive to the busy, work-filled lives of our participants. And a couple of times each year we use a donated storefront in the South End as a space for Kabbalat Shabbat [Friday evening] services.[1]

The focus of the enterprise is worship and an in-depth, intensive study of sacred texts, along with social justice activities. What is critical is participants' personal ownership and direction of the project as they are gently guided by its rabbinic leader (who is paid by Temple Israel). Because of the age range of most participants, the community is transitory. Some have moved out of the area and some have become members of Temple Israel.

Lessons Learned about Public Space Judaism Events

1. Some affiliated people—who may not be part of the target audience—will undoubtedly attend Public Space Judaism events. But the focus of recruitment efforts should be on those previously unaffiliated—that's the target population.
2. Only about a third of the people encountered from the target audience will be interested in moving forward on the path of engagement during the first year of follow-up activities and events. The other two-thirds will take an additional year or two.
3. Families with young children tend to access Judaism through their children at holiday time.
4. For Public Space Judaism events to be most effective, they have to take place on numerous occasions throughout the year and be dispersed throughout the wider community.
5. Public Space Judaism events raise the profile of the sponsoring institution. As a result, soliciting funds (but not at the events themselves) from community members outside the sponsoring institution becomes easier.

Reflection and Discussion Questions for Synagogue Leaders

1. How can synagogue leaders transform those events already planned into Public Space Judaism events?
2. How can we reallocate our human and fiscal resources to make Public Space Judaism events a priority?
3. Who among our active participants and members would be most effective planning and implementing such events?

Public Space Judaism events are only one way of turning your institution inside out. But they are proven, effective entry vehicles for finding people and engaging them. They are not meant to replace more intensive programs or activities for those who already part of your community. But they are a good way to begin the process of turning your institution completely inside out.

CHAPTER 3

The Marketplace
of Ideas

The central concept of this chapter emerges from the aforementioned notion that the young Jews in our midst are the first generation of fully American, American Jews. Thus, their experience of America and Judaism is far different from those of generations past. Just as Jews have achieved a status equal to nearly all others in the United States, it can similarly be said that Judaism as a religious philosophy or ideology has achieved such a status and thereby has entered into what can best be described as the marketplace of ideas. Like the economic free market, the notion of *marketplace of ideas* is a rationale for the free and unfettered expression of ideas. Just as competition is said to yield a better product in the economic market, it is assumed that truths will emerge from the marketplace of ideas. Thus, the marketplace of ideas is applied to public discourse as well as freedom of the press and patent law, and it is the foundation of liberal democracy. The notion was said to be first introduced by the philosopher John Stuart Mill in 1859.

Judaism and Jewish philosophy is taking its rightful place among other philosophies that attract the attention of the American public, such as ancient Greek philosophy or the philosophy-theology of Eastern religions. When ideas are out in the open, anyone can study such ideas or engage with them without feeling that they have to become a member of that civilization or religious group. In the case of Judaism, the public can study Judaism without feeling compelled to convert to Judaism, and Judaism itself is available outside the limits of Jewish institutions.

This openness of ideas, what might be called Open Source Judaism, is what allows the popular music star Madonna to develop an interest in kabbalah without any interest in converting to Judaism. Her interest in kabbalah took her to Israel in 2004 (and then again in 2007), where she led a group of two thousand fellow kabbalah students (presumably not Jewish) during the Second Intifada, a time when few were visiting Israel. It was rumored that she was even purchasing a home in Rosh Pina, very near the ancient city of Safed, the heart of mysticism in Israel. Madonna never expressed an interest in converting to Judaism, although her interest in one form of Jewish philosophy did spill over into advocacy for the land of Israel.

Another celebrity attracted to Judaism is singer Justin Bieber. This young heartthrob made a commitment to recite the Shema blessing (which observant Jews recite during morning and evening prayer services and just prior to going to sleep) prior to each concert. Christina Aguilera, another singer, arranged for a traditional ritual circumcision for her son. And Victoria Beckham (aka Posh Spice) had the Hebrew phrase from the biblical Song of Songs 6:3 ("I am my beloved's and my beloved is mine, the one who grazes in the lilies") tattooed along her spine. Apparently, her husband, the soccer star David Beckham, had the line tattooed as well, among his many tattoos. The extent of Jewish philosophical and cultural influence on non-Jews is quite extensive. One translator (working mostly from Hebrew into English) tells me that she receives requests daily for translations of pithy sayings, primarily so that her inquirers can have these texts tattooed onto their skin in Hebrew.

While not as profound as the influence of Jewish thought on American society and individual Americans, a similar influence can be seen in popular Jewish culture and ethnic cuisine. Consider as one example how quickly the bagel went from a (New York) Jewish food to an American fast food (in direct competition with the ubiquitous McDonald's). And now hummus and falafel have followed suit, both in the supermarket and in stand-alone fast-food restaurants such as Maoz or Crisp, both of which are making their way from the coasts to the center of the country.

As a result of Judaism's operating in the open market, many people will be interested in its ideology or culture. Of course, the presence of Judaism in the open market will also mean that the number of people interested in converting to Judaism will increase, but the majority of those interested in Judaism will have no interest in converting. Nevertheless, the synagogue community—since conversion is currently only a religious rite, managed by rabbis—must be prepared to deal with this phenomenon and respond to it. Thus, synagogues must be prepared to deal with people's interest in Judaism both because it is a cultural phenomenon and because it might be a solution to the problem of demographic decline.

Noted sociologist Steven M. Cohen and I have proposed an alternative for people who are interested in Judaism but who are not interested in conversion, especially through religious means. We would call these individuals *Jews by culture*, taking a cue for the name from the idea of *Jews by choice*, the popular euphemism used to designate converts to Judaism. We do not see those who identify themselves as Jews by culture as undertaking a process for conversion (which had been proposed by Yossi Beilin, a left-wing Israeli politician and former member of Knesset, Israel's parliament). Instead, we see the approach to this segment of those interested in Judaism enough to become Jews by culture as more a means of affirming Jewish ideas. The idea does take a cue from the book of Ruth: "Your people will be my people" (Ruth 1:16). This biblical text is often referenced by people who convert to Judaism. But the verse goes on to say, "Your God will be my God," which is relevant to those who convert to Judaism but perhaps not relevant to those who are simply affirming select Jewish ideas.

Regardless of the result—conversion, affirmation, or just plain interest in Judaism—the notion that Judaism has entered the marketplace of ideas will directly affect the role of the synagogue, and the Jewish community, in responding to individuals who are interested only in cultural Judaism. Cultural Judaism—not to be confused with humanism or a secular Judaism that affirms Jewish religion without God—will challenge the synagogue, which formerly stood as the primary vehicle for teaching Judaism to the local community.

Rabbi Irwin Kula, copresident of Clal, calls Judaism a technology. He argues that Judaism is no longer a set of beliefs that tribally binds Jewish people together. Rather, it is a practice—among others—that can help human beings become more human. Because of this expanded notion of Judaism as a technology rather than a tribe, Judaism has become a popular asset in the marketplace of ideas. Kula argues that those who see Judaism in this way—and therefore agree with him—are the ones who sustain humanity and that Judaism is of interest to all. He even goes so far as to claim that the extent to which we may resonate with individual mitzvot (sacred commandments) or rituals is to be measured by one question: Does it actually help the individual develop an understanding of the truth of one's life? He uses the basic ritual of affixing the mezuzah (on the doorposts of one's home) as a poignant example. He argues that the ritual is fundamentally unimportant. It only becomes important if the mezuzah placed on a doorpost of a particular room suggests that one behaves appropriately in that space.

Most Jews who affix the mezuzah do so without much thought. It is almost like a housewarming ritual. Although the practice has ritual authority to it, most people view it as a simple statement announcing "Here lives a Jewish family." Because of the connection between the mezuzah affixed to the door that is the entry to the house and the family that lives in the house, the placement of a mezuzah is not a simple decision for an intermarried family because its presence implies something about who lives inside the house. Instead, the ritual act of affixing a mezuzah is usually carefully discussed, because the placement of a mezuzah for all to see does declare that the family inside the home is Jewish—or has chosen Judaism as its religious identification.

While this notion of Judaism in the marketplace of ideas is not necessarily linked to conversion, as noted above, some people will indeed be interested in conversion to Judaism as a result of their new exposure to Judaism. Historically, Jewish authorities have been reluctant to provide easy access to Judaism through conversion. Contemporary rabbis have bought in to the mainstream rabbinic tradition of refusing the potential candidate three times before even entertaining any interest in his or her conversion. Here's the irony: At a time when interest in Judaism is increasing, converting to Judaism is becoming more difficult. The difficulty is primarily a result of the religious right wing's influence, particularly the chief rabbinate in Israel, who constantly question the conversions supervised by individual rabbis and seek to invalidate them. Thus, many rabbis, including Orthodox rabbis, are attempting to evade the threat of invalidation or being challenged by refusing to convert anyone to Judaism. Rather than finding a way to make it happen, they are avoiding the issue entirely. This is the wrong approach, especially at a time of demographic decline and decreasing engagement by the synagogue. There is persuasive anecdotal evidence that those who convert to Judaism become active participants in the synagogue and the entire Jewish community.

A few years ago, as my organization, the Jewish Outreach Institute, advocated the implementation of Public Space Judaism (as discussed in chapter 2), one of the Home Depot stores on Long Island helped its customers build traditional sukkot (plural of sukkah), the temporary booths used in the celebration of the

Sukkot fall harvest festival. While the Home Depot's assistance in building a sukkah might be construed as a literal entry of Jewish ritual into the marketplace, and not just the marketplace of ideas, the building of a traditional sukkah is really a high-barrier ritual. Even among those who are traditionally observant of Jewish rituals, the building of a sukkah at one's home takes a back seat to some of the other lower-barrier rituals. However, a few years ago, Reboot, an innovative Jewish organization whose goal is to engage millennial Jews through innovative programs, initiated a contest among architects and design students to build an innovative sukkah (following the traditional requirements for dimensions and the like). The best ten examples of these sukkot were built in Union Square, a busy public area in New York City. The designs were created by Jews and non-Jews, and while the sukkot theoretically could have been used for ritual celebration, they were not. Instead, they were designed for the thousands of visitors to Union Square to view and enjoy. They were not used to engage the viewers beyond the experience of simply viewing. Planners didn't seem to want to use the sukkot to draw viewers into the Jewish community. This kind of public sukkah-building has been replicated in other cities as well.

For Jews, the building of sukkot represents two notions. First, sukkot reflect the temporary housing of the ancient Israelites during their sojourn from Egypt to Canaan. Second, they reflect the protective huts that harvesters use in the field when they rest during harvest season, because leaving the field for a break and returning to it afterward wastes too much time. Beyond these two ideas, sukkot represent the fragility of life. They represent that connection between humans and the environment. While Jews may resonate with all these ideas related to sukkot, non-Jews, in particular, often find these latter ideas appealing.

When the hip-hop artist Jay Z opened his eight-day concert tour at the new Barclays Center in Brooklyn, New York, he chose to light a candle in a Hanukkah menorah *(hanukiyah)* each night.

Hanukkah was to be celebrated two months after his tour, so this was not really a celebration of Hanukkah. And Jay Z isn't Jewish. Nevertheless, something of the Jewish holiday culture appealed to him—perhaps it was the message of freedom personified by the light—and the eight days of Hanukkah represented in the menorah were a perfect match for his eight-day concert tour. True, Hanukkah has become the national Jewish holiday (some say the Jewish Christmas) because of its proximity in the calendar to Christmas, and the festivals' roots may emerge from the same winter solstice celebration. But their journeys through history took them to far different theological conclusions. Nonetheless, Jay Z chose this vehicle to celebrate his concerts and the opening of the Barclays Center. Had the menorah and Hanukkah not been accessible to him in the marketplace of ideas, he probably wouldn't have selected them for the message he wanted to promote via his concert.

Kavod v'Nichum (literally, "Honor and Comfort") is a national organization devoted to the Jewish preparation of bodies following death and prior to burial. These procedures are generally undertaken by local organizations—often synagogue-based—called the Chevra Kaddisha (Holy Society). Its members are considered to be among the most righteous, since they perform sacred tasks for which there is no chance for reward from the individual for whom the task is being provided. As such, the acts are considered totally selfless (referred to as *hesed v'emet* in Hebrew). While Kavod v'Nichum has been training members of local Chevra Kaddisha groups for several years, it has recently ventured into new territory. Through a program called the Gamaliel Institute, members of Kavod v'Nichum are now teaching a growing number of people outside the Jewish community who say that the Jewish procedures of body preparation appeal to them because of the dignity that traditional Judaism accords the body. Such interest would not have been apparent some years ago, nor would such an organization have interest in sharing such skills with the general community. This is another prime example of Judaism entering the marketplace of ideas with its emphasis on human dignity even after the person has died, and of the desire among those who are not Jewish to take on rituals that would have previously been restricted to Jews.

Competing in a Free Market Economy

Like most Jewish communal institutions, the synagogue has been used to operating within the parameters of the Jewish communal world. Its financial support came from membership dues and philanthropic contributions. While it might have perceived itself as competing with other synagogues, with other Jewish communal institutions, or with secular delights for the attention of its members, it has never really competed in the open market to engage people or attract them to Judaism or Jewish ideas. When Jews were forced by societal limitations to stay inside the Jewish community, then the synagogue became the primary institution in which Jews could gain access to "all things Jewish." That is no longer the case. Jews can access Judaism in a variety of places. Thus, if the synagogue wants to follow this move into the marketplace of ideas, then it will be entering the free market economy. A free market economy is a competitive environment based on supply and demand with little or no control by the government. In addition, such an economy features a free pricing system. Now that synagogues are in the marketplace, they are competing with other institutions that share "retail space" with them. They succeed or fail based simply on whether people "buy" their product and they realize a profit.

A large number of institutions and projects, especially in the educational sphere, are developing as for-profit enterprises. One of the most popular Jewish enterprises today is JDate, a for-profit undertaking. But JDate is not alone in this new environment.

As the number of intermarriages has increased (discussed more fully in chapter 4), the question of where to bury a non-Jewish spouse has inevitably emerged, along with a variety of other issues relevant to the burial and mourning of non-Jewish relatives. As a result, a debate ensued among synagogue leaders concerning whether to bury a non-Jewish spouse in a Jewish cemetery. At the same time, so-called commercial (or for-profit) cemeteries with names like Mount Lebanon or Beth Israel immediately responded to the expressed need, thereby undermining opportunities for the synagogue and other Jewish communal institutions that owned or operated cemeteries to respond, because these institutions require more time to process such issues. Some are still discussing the issue! Nonetheless, others have decided to provide burial plots for non-Jewish spouses. Some have even gone so far as to provide space for the burial of other non-Jewish family members. These cemeteries operate within the Jewish community, even if they are for-profit enterprises.

As part of the economic challenge suggested by operating in a free market economy, many synagogues are now looking for income-producing vehicles to support themselves. For example, one synagogue is exploring how it can harness solar energy to sell to the local electric grid and thereby reduce its own electrical costs. Others have become landlords, renting out space on a regular basis to programs and institutions that have nothing to do with the synagogue or Jewish life, going so far as to purchase property in order to rent it out for a profit. Another synagogue has partnered with a for-profit child care franchise to help develop and implement its preschool program. Such synagogues now understand that they are competing in a marketplace very different from the one they had been involved in before. While it has been common for some time to use recognizable brands to increase the appeal of traditional programming—for example, some synagogues promote Starbucks Shabbat, which really means Starbucks coffee is being served during the Oneg

Shabbat, or fellowship hour, following services—synagogues are now trying to use those brands to actually draw people into their institutions. This would mean opening a free-standing kiosk for Starbucks (coffee) or a Subway (sandwiches) or a Rita's (ices) in the synagogue. Megachurches have taken this approach for some time in order to create a consumer-friendly, mall-like atmosphere in the church.

In their rush to be competitive and profitable, synagogue leaders may be missing the message that brand recognition is teaching us. Often the product is secondary to the context in which the product is either purchased or consumed. Howard Schultz, CEO of Starbucks, speaks about the "third space" as the place outside the home or work environment where people gather to socialize. He has successfully turned his stores into such an environment. Thus, synagogues should be pursuing for-profit vehicles not simply because they may be income producing. Rather, they should be pursuing these vehicles because they provide a context for building community at the same time.

This is what Makor (a gathering place for millennials) tried to do in New York City's Upper West Side. Supported by mega-philanthropist Michael Steinhardt, the visionaries at Makor attempted to create a gathering place for young Jews, especially those unaffiliated with Jewish institutions such as synagogues. Makor included a performance space, a (kosher) café, an auditorium for film screenings, and some classrooms. However, it was built on a side street rather than an avenue. As a result, people were less likely to stumble upon it. Makor attempted to create its own brand name for the facility and the café, rather than borrowing an already recognized brand. It lasted for a few years before being fully absorbed into the 92nd Street Y. The 92nd Street Y then used the Makor space for its regular programming and moved Makor's programming to a new location in Tribeca (also in New York City), where there are few Jewish communal services and a growing number of young Jews and families with young children. Had I been responsible for the original Makor, I probably would not have spent money to purchase and convert three brownstones into one building. Instead, I would have chosen a well-known brand with available franchises, like Starbucks or something similar, and rented space above it for performances, classes, or presentations. And I would have rented the space—rather than purchasing it—to avoid the albatross of extensive overhead and to gain the flexibility to abandon it for other spaces when the need arose. However, Makor did well in its concerts and has replicated that success and expanded upon it in its new location. Nonetheless, it was recently closed and resources placed back into the flagship institution uptown.

Now is not the first time in history that synagogues have sought for-profit enterprises. Synagogue gift shops abounded in the last generation, especially in communities that didn't have Judaica shops. And these gift shops seemed to be in concert with the values and mission of the synagogue. But as synagogues approach other vehicles to finance their enterprise, they might be accused of mission drift. As a result, synagogues might do well to approach any for-profit enterprise from the perspective of expanding or complementing their mission.

Ultimately, however, synagogues will have to change their approach to the marketplace. No longer can they rest on the laurels of previous successes or prior generations. Much like successful kosher restaurants that know they have to appeal to the general public and not just to the kosher observant population if they are to prosper, synagogues will have to recognize that they are now competing in an open marketplace for the attention and the resources of their members or potential members.

Ten Things about Judaism and the Marketplace of Ideas

1. Jewish thought can enrich the lives of people, whether or not the people are Jewish.

2. There are many access points to Jewish thought outside the religious realm.
3. Jewish values, particularly because they are often manifest in concrete ways, are of particular interest to those in the marketplace of ideas.
4. For Jewish thought to speak to the masses, it has to be accessible and cannot remain hidden within the walls of Jewish communal institutions.
5. Like Jewish thought, Jewish culture has also found its place in the marketplace.
6. The influence of Jewish thought and Jewish culture is particularly apparent in popular media.
7. The culture of so-called open source, made possible by the Internet, is ideal for sharing Jewish ideas in the marketplace of ideas. As a result, they can be accessed by all.
8. The marketplace of ideas is pluralistic and knows no boundaries or limitations.
9. All ideas are subject to scrutiny and criticism in the marketplace. Thus, they have to stand on their own merit.
10. There is no ownership of ideas in the marketplace.

The Kabbalah Centre

I have been unable to find a synagogue or Jewish communal institution that has really moved itself—or even a part of itself—into what I have referred to as the marketplace of ideas. This marketplace is one that encourages the free and democratic expression of ideas. Rabbi Irwin Kula has done so indirectly through Clal, the institution he serves as copresident, and its Rabbis Without Borders training program for rabbis who are interested in sharing Jewish wisdom beyond Jewish institutional confines, but no synagogue has taken such a step. As a result, I have decided to focus this brief case study on the Kabbalah Centre, which calls itself a spiritual and educational center for the study of Lurianic Kabbalah (named for Rabbi Isaac Luria, a preeminent kabbalist of the sixteenth century). I recognize that the institution is considered a bit controversial by many people, and some will argue that it is cultish. I mean to neither celebrate its success nor denigrate it for any of its shortcomings. I simply want to use it as an example of a Jewish organization that has successfully and demonstrably moved Jewish thought—in particular, kabbalah—into the marketplace of ideas by attracting to a specific area of Jewish thought those who aren't Jewish and who have no interest in converting to Judaism.

Rabbi Philip Berg, formerly a businessman, joined his wife in establishing and developing the center. They started with a single location, and there are now forty branches of the Kabbalah Centre around the world. Clearly, the Bergs have been successful at moving Judaism into the marketplace of ideas and building an institution there. And I wonder why other institutions have not done so. While there have been many high profile individuals attracted to the Kabbalah Centre, the person who has gained the most attention is perhaps Madonna. She has been so enamored by the work of the Kabbalah Centre and its teachings that she has even brought a group of devotees to Israel, all of whom are attracted to kabbalah but have no desire to convert to Judaism or really any apparent interest in the wide expanse of Jewish knowledge. What is perhaps most important about the work of the Kabbalah Centre is how Berg has taken an area of Jewish thought that is dense and esoteric and made it accessible for the masses.

LESSONS LEARNED IN THE MARKETPLACE OF IDEAS

1. Jewish communal institutions are wary of Jewish thought being presented in the marketplace by institutions that are not part of the traditional Jewish communal landscape.

2. Personality cults can rise up around teachers of Jewish thought in the marketplace.
3. Popular Jewish thought is not necessarily the area that will attract most people. Sometimes esoteric Jewish thought, in which many Jewish communal leaders are not expert, is what will attract people.
4. Because of the relationship between the marketplace of ideas and a free market economy, Jewish communal institutions are often unsure how to change their approach to program in order to operate successfully in both.
5. Those institutions operating outside the Jewish communal structure will not be considered insiders unless the community is open to the notion of a marketplace of ideas.

Reflection and Discussion Questions for Synagogue Leaders

1. If people are attracted to Judaism and want to convert to Judaism, are we willing to make conversion more accessible? If so, how would we do so?
2. How can we allow people who are attracted to Jewish ideas to engage our community institutions even if they don't want to convert to Judaism?
3. What program changes need to happen for our institutions to effectively share Jewish thought in the marketplace?

The notion of operating in a marketplace that is not defined by explicit boundaries that protect Judaism from outsiders is quite challenging for most Jewish communal institutions and their leadership. If Jewish leaders respond to widespread interest in Jewish thought and culture, however, we can hope to gradually benefit all humanity.

CHAPTER 4

Intermarriage as an Opportunity, Not a Problem

I believe that intermarriage is among the most important domestic issues facing the North American Jewish community today. I also believe that the wisdom with which we respond to intermarriage and those who have intermarried will determine the landscape of the Jewish community we bequeath to our children and grandchildren. Unlike so many other social phenomena that are out of our immediate control, including whom our adult children marry, every individual can indeed directly affect our community's response to the issue of intermarriage by how we individually respond to those who are intermarried (defined simply as a marriage between someone who is Jewish and someone whose faith of origin is a religion other than Judaism and has not converted to Judaism).

For most of my childhood and adult life—and certainly for the years I was in rabbinical school—the attitude regarding intermarriage of those in Jewish synagogue leadership positions could be likened to a war. There was no place in the synagogue and in the community for people who were intermarried. Parents of intermarried adults—and even their siblings—were embarrassed and guilt-ridden. Needless to say, they were unwelcoming to the non-Jewish family member and his or her family of origin. This was not limited to the more traditionally observant.

It included liberal families as well. While some families went to the extreme of sitting shiva (the seven-day period of mourning for the deceased), they often disinherited children and excluded them from family gatherings and life-cycle events. Rabbis railed against intermarriage from the pulpit with horrific allusions to the Holocaust. In places where it might be politically incorrect to offer a blatant anti-intermarriage message, the implicit warning against intermarriage was just as clear. Interdating was prohibited among many families and discouraged in youth groups and religious school classrooms. And some synagogues barred even the Jewish partner in an intermarriage from synagogue membership. Needless to say, in those congregations, non-Jewish partners were not welcome at all.

Whatever the motivation for the war on intermarriage, I have come to believe it has been a failure. Jewish communal leadership in North America has no influence over whom their children marry, especially in a society that promotes equality for all. Intermarriage reflects the democratic culture that is the hallmark of the United States. And even if there were no intermarriages from this day forward, what do we do with the 1.25 million intermarried Jewish families who are already part of the community? So many of us have spent too much time pushing people away. It is time to embrace people's choices and the people who made them. Rather than seeing intermarriage as Judaism's biggest problem, I see intermarriage as our greatest opportunity. Reaching those who have intermarried will not only mitigate natural demographic decline in the United States, it will actually help grow the North American Jewish community. Thus, it is time to welcome individuals who have intermarried—and particularly their non-Jewish partners and family members—into the orbit of the synagogue.

Intermarriage is neither a new phenomenon in the Jewish community nor restricted to it. Intermarriage is a North American phenomenon. Yet, it affects the Jewish community more significantly than perhaps any other because of the small size of the North American— and world—Jewish population, especially in comparison to the Christian population. Admittedly, the rate for marriages between Jews and those from other faith backgrounds in this generation is higher than ever before. But it is not the direct result of Jews wanting to marry someone who is not Jewish. Rather, the increase can be attributed to a willingness on the part of those who are not Jewish to marry someone who is Jewish. In previous generations, people who were not Jewish were not interested in marrying Jews. Why would someone want to marry into a populace that was vulnerable and at risk? But as noted previously, Jews have transcended their vulnerability and have become quintessentially American. Consequently, Jews have emerged as desirable life partners. Jews don't marry those of other religious backgrounds in order to run away from Judaism. They are not "marrying out." In this open society, an individual simply meets someone, falls in love, and decides to spend his or her life with that person.

The Torah of Welcoming

While there are many reasons to welcome non-Jews who have married someone who is Jewish into the Jewish community, the most persuasive reason to adopt a welcoming posture toward those of other religious backgrounds stems from the foundational values of Judaism itself. Placed right in the center of the Torah—in a section called the Holiness Code, because it sets the standard for Jewish behavior (and was therefore historically among the first texts taught to children as they began their Jewish education)— come lines that have framed Jewish attitudes for centuries: "The stranger that lives with you shall be to you like the native, and you shall love him [or her] as yourself; for you were strangers in the land of Egypt. I am the Lord your God" (Lev. 19:34). By adding that divine seal at the end of directive, the Torah text communicates its message quite strongly, making clear the origin of this instruction. There seems to be no question about how we are to act, and this signature text is meant as a core value.

But the instruction in the Torah to be welcoming is insufficient. A single statement is not enough to guide people on such an important moral directive, even with the divine affirmation attached to such guidance. So the instruction is repeated more than thirty times in various places and in various contexts throughout the Torah, reiterated more often than any other commandment. The value of welcoming and loving the stranger is so basic to the formation of the Jewish religious psyche that it is emphasized even more frequently than are the laws of Shabbat or the kosher dietary laws. This means that the simple act of being welcoming to others, particularly strangers in our midst, is more important than the various ritual acts emphasized by the various religious streams of Judaism.

Why does the Jewish sacred tradition direct us to welcome those "strangers" who are in our midst? Because we remember what it was like to be strangers when we were enslaved in Egypt. Because we have not forgotten what it was like to be strangers when we were scattered to all the nations of the world, wandering through history without a sense of belonging. Because we understand that the most humane and *human* way to express the covenantal relationship with God is by reaching out to others and welcoming them in.

While some people argue that the strictures of halacha (Jewish law) demand their resistance to intermarriage and their rejection of those who are intermarried, I believe that they are actually camouflaging their fear of strangers by claiming their inflexibility is rooted in their adherence to Jewish law. Some of this fear is justified. A read of Jewish history provides evidence of anti-Jewish sentiment and activity among strangers. But such clandestine activity against Jewish people is a thing of the past.

Fear of spies in the community has not been something the North American Jewish community has worried about for the last couple of generations. What is really preventing synagogue members from welcoming people who are intermarried is the culture of the synagogue, and that has to change. Synagogue culture is hard to describe. It may be even harder to change. If the synagogue were a sporting event, then its culture would be found more in the viewing stands than on the playing field. Thus, synagogue culture is more evident in the behavior of congregants than in the message coming from the pulpit. However, permission to behave in an unwelcoming way—however unconscious the behavior may be—could be interpreted by congregants as coming directly from the clergy. This culture has to change if we are to grow the Jewish community. The only way to be faithful to Jewish tradition—rooted in the Torah—is to welcome into synagogue engagement those who have traditionally been marginalized.

Welcoming In

The work of outreach to people who are intermarried is not difficult. While it is true that most people in the synagogue community are at best ambivalent about intermarriage, few families, regardless of religious denomination, do not have family members who are intermarried. Most of the time these intermarriages are in their immediate families. So when we speak about those who are intermarried, we are no longer talking about *them*. We are now talking about *us*. Thus, a synagogue that does not welcome individuals who are intermarried is actually preventing members of our own families from participating in synagogue life.

While we use the term *intermarriage* to refer to a wide spectrum of people and family configurations, those who are intermarried can be divided into four main categories. While demographers and sociologists will argue over the percentage of people who populate each segment of the intermarried, for our purposes it is important only to identify the overarching trends and not quibble about percentage points. The distinction of percentage points may be important for scientific exactitude, but it is not helpful in a discussion about how to respond to intermarriage or how to welcome intermarried families into the synagogue.

Of the four main categories of those who are intermarried, the one group that is already recognized as inside the Jewish community are families whose adult members have made the choice to raise Jewish children. This accounts for about 25 to 35 percent of intermarried families. These intermarried families are found primarily in Reform synagogues. (The Reform movement claims that about 33 percent of its members are intermarried and about 50 percent are families with children in its religious schools.) Unlike most other Jewish leaders who call these families interfaith families, I am bold enough to call these families Jewish families. I do so because the religion of the family is Judaism, regardless of the fact that one adult parent is not Jewish. In fact, those who are intermarried and actively involved in the Jewish community look like everyone else who is inmarried and an enthusiastic participant. While the Jewish community may think that intermarried families wear their so-called intermarriage on their sleeves as a shibboleth, this is not the case. Moreover, intermarried families do not view the rest of the world through their intermarriage. It is often only when forced into a position in which their differences are made visible, such as a worship context when others are covering themselves with a tallit (prayer shawl), that the differences become what sociologists call socially visible. This may be the first time others realize that a couple is intermarried or that one partner isn't Jewish.

The second category of people who are intermarried are those raising children in a different faith, primarily a Christian faith, although an increasing number of intermarriages are occurring between American Jews and those of faiths other than Christianity. Even in this group, however, many parents want to expose their children to the heritage of the Jewish parent and grandparents.

And a third group of people who are intermarried are raising children in two faiths. This latter group is doing more than just exposing their children to holidays (such as Hanukkah and Christmas) in both religions. Rather, their approach is a concerted effort to school children in both faiths and to encourage them to attend religious services of both faith groups as well. Often they encourage their children to make their own religious choices when they come of age. These two groups make up about a second quarter to third of interfaith families.

The largest group of intermarried families—and perhaps the most significant target for engagement by the synagogue—are those raising their children in what I call American civil religion, that is, families who observe Thanksgiving, the Fourth of July, and the like, with a smattering of Hanukkah and Christmas, Easter and Passover. But this group—up to about 50 percent according to most estimates—is quite different from those who are attempting to raise their children in two religions. As a matter of fact, they look like most Americans who do not attend a house of worship and whose holiday celebrations are secular and centered on family. Too often, however, the synagogue writes this population off as unreachable primarily because the family may have a Christmas tree in their home. For the majority of Jews, a Christmas tree in the homes of intermarried families is interpreted to mean that Judaism is irrelevant to their identities. However, for these families, the tree may be just a tree. It may represent a family celebration of a holiday rather than an affirmation of the religious sentiments contained in the holiday itself. And while I do not advocate such a secular mix of religious cultures, I am not prepared to write off these families as not part of the

Jewish community. Thus, they are members of the synagogue community that I argued for in chapter 2.

Some critics will argue against my view that synagogues need to be open and welcoming to intermarried couples, since these critics believe that intermarriage necessarily leads to the diminution of Judaism and of the Jewish people. However, I have often seen a so-called intermarriage evolve into a Jewish family where there would not necessarily have been one had the Jewish partner in that relationship married another Jew. And we know that if two Jews marry one another, they can create one Jewish family. But if these two Jews marry people who are not Jewish, then they can possibly create two Jewish families—with twice as many children as one family alone. If we don't open our synagogues to those who are intermarried, we can't blame them for not wanting to participate in the life of the synagogue or for not sending their children to our schools. We have seen a sufficient number of synagogues that are open to those who are intermarried and that allow intermarried families to freely participate in them, such that their children are more likely to develop a secure Jewish identity as a result.

Interdating

Interdating is usually presented as a concomitant of the intermarriage issue. And just as most synagogues over the last several generations have taken a strict position with regard to intermarriage, these synagogues have taken a similarly stringent position regarding interdating. However, as the average marrying age has increased in the United States, dating issues should become less a concern to the educational programs of the synagogue. If men who marry in the United States typically marry at the age of twenty-nine (a year earlier for women), according to the U.S.

Census, they are most likely not living with their parents at the time, not living in the city in which they were raised, and not socializing in the network of their childhood. Thus, any influence of the institutions of childhood on one's choice of marriage partner, including the social pressures placed upon a young person by his or her parents, is rather limited.

However misguided, synagogues use what is at their disposal to discourage interdating, thinking that if they can dissuade people from interdating, then they can limit the number of intermarriages. Most education concerning interdating has been directed toward teenagers, particularly those in high school. Yet most kids are certainly not marrying right out of high school or even immediately after college. Moreover, kids in high school go out in groups more than they date. And even the critics of intermarriage are not advocating that their children limit their social groups to only Jews. If synagogues are going to persist and speak to kids about their future families, then I would like synagogues to move the conversation from whom they plan to marry to how they plan to raise their children.

The Rights of Intermarried Families

Interdating is not the only issue in the spectrum of issues related to intermarriage and the synagogue that will require synagogue leaders to rethink the immovable positions they have held. For example, in the United States, the right to vote is often considered to be the battleground for equality. That is what the women's suffrage movement was all about. It was also a primary motivation behind the civil rights movement in the 1960s. Currently, the right to vote is a critical issue in the arguments over the rights of undocumented immigrants. There is no reason why intermarried family members should not have voting rights in the synagogue.

The argument that people are afraid those who are not Jewish will be able to vote on the destiny of the synagogue has no merit, since individuals who cast their lot with the Jewish people by marrying a Jew and participating in the synagogue community have already demonstrated an interest in the future of the Jewish people. Why else would they be raising Jewish children? Some synagogues have developed a mechanism to avoid the issue by providing voting rights by member units—sometimes called family units, however the family is configured—rather than by individuals. While few people are rushing to secure voting rights at the synagogue, providing intermarried families with voting rights in the synagogue is still an important statement about equality and inclusion that has to be made. If we want the synagogue to remain relevant to the population of families with young children, then we have to extend voting rights to the majority of them—those who are intermarried.

Access to Leadership Roles

Access to synagogue leadership positions also has to be opened up to intermarried families, particularly to adult members of the family unit who are not Jewish. In some synagogues, those who are not Jewish and married to someone who is Jewish are permitted to serve on committees but only committees that do not make any ritual decisions. In most cases, the partner who is not Jewish is not permitted to sit on the board or to serve as president of the synagogue. If we want the volunteer leadership of the institution to represent and reflect its constituency, then this too must change. Moreover, if a growing number of synagogue families are intermarried and synagogues successfully attract them, yet they are not permitted to rise to leadership positions, then leadership will only be open to a minority of synagogue members.

Life-Cycle Events

Perhaps the most important issue for intermarried families—and the role of the non-Jewish adult in the synagogue—concerns life-cycle events. As noted in chapter 2, most synagogues limit themselves to four major life-cycle areas: birth, coming of age, family life, and end of life. Synagogues have adopted a wide range of policies concerning interfaith families and these life-cycle events. Most of them lean toward being restrictive. Non-Jewish partners are not permitted to participate significantly in most of these life-cycle events. Perhaps they may be able to offer an English reading or make a presentation, as long as they are accompanied by Jewish partner. But very few synagogues afford them the same ritual privileges as their Jewish partners.

Whether rabbis should officiate at the wedding of interfaith couples is among the most contentious issues related to these four life-cycle arenas. While some rabbis—Reform and Reconstructionist—have the freedom to make their own choices as to whether they are willing to officiate at interfaith weddings, most rabbis are prohibited by their rabbinical associations (connected with their religious movements and reflecting the positions taken by their respective religious movements) from doing so. I don't want synagogues to transcend the restrictions placed on them by their movements. Nor do I want synagogues (and their rabbis) to exceed the limits of their conscience. However, I do believe that we can stretch our comfort levels beyond the current practices and find ways to serve intermarried families so that they can mark their life-cycle events within the synagogue community. In so doing, we will fulfill the obligation of becoming an inclusive Jewish community, and those who join our ranks will benefit from the blessings of such an association. (More on "Why Be Jewish?" in chapter 7.)

Adult Children of Intermarriage

The natural result of an open attitude toward intermarriage will be more children in our community who are the products of these relationships. In fact, the fastest growing segment of the American Jewish population is what is often described as adult children of intermarriage. Based on the general programming of the synagogue that I read about, synagogues do not seem to be interested in this population. If they are interested, nothing seems to be designed to reach this target population. Some of these adult children may choose to call themselves half Jews, a descriptor rejected by Jewish scholarship. And while that is technically correct—there is really no category in Jewish law such as half Jew—this claim to a self-identifying moniker does help some of them as they struggle with their identity and where they fit in the synagogue community. Irrespective of what they call themselves, the synagogue needs to reach out and welcome them in.

Rather than dimming the colors of the Jewish religion, intermarriage has the potential to add color to the richly textured tapestry of American Jewish life. There is virtually no domestic issue facing the North American Jewish community—short of perhaps the survival of the modern state of Israel—that does not have some relationship to the issue of intermarriage. The majority of families that include people of color in the Jewish community have intermarriage in their ranks. Members of the lesbian, gay, bisexual, or transgendered (LGBT) community have a higher intermarriage rate than do other population groups. And the Jewish community is working hard to include these population segments. A welcoming approach to people who are intermarried is indispensable if synagogues are to reclaim their status as the central Jewish institution. We should reach out to those who are intermarried because it will enhance the size of the community.

We should reach out to those who are intermarried because those who are intermarried—and their entire families—will benefit from participating in Jewish life. And we should reach out to those who are intermarried because it is the right—the Jewish—thing to do.

Ten Things We Know about Intermarriage

1. There are individuals who want to divide the community into those who are intermarried and those who are inmarried. The real divide is between people who are engaged with our community and people who are unengaged.
2. The organized Jewish community would like to have us believe that intermarriage is about "marrying out." However, intermarriage *can* be just as much about others "marrying in."
3. The majority of American *wedding ceremonies* that involve one partner who is Jewish are intermarriages. Similarly, most *marriages* containing a Jewish spouse are intermarried households, totaling over one million households. The result is more intermarried households than inmarried households.
4. Intermarriage is a demographically driven phenomenon. The larger and more concentrated the local Jewish community, the lower the rate of intermarriage.
5. Different segments of the community intermarry at different rates. And more intermarriages are second marriages than first marriages.
6. Adult children of intermarriage are the coming majority. Already, 45 percent of the students who identify Jewishly on the college campus come from interfaith families, even though national studies claim only about one-third of children in interfaith households are raised as Jews. I boldly call a Jewish household any household that raises Jewish

children, even if one adult partner in that household is not Jewish.

7. At any given time, the majority (85 percent) of interfaith households do not affiliate with institutions in the North American Jewish community. Those who do affiliate are playing important roles in our institutions, especially synagogues. What often keeps them out is institutional culture rather than halakha (Jewish law).

8. Programs of Jewish education and identity development may not determine whether a child marries someone who is Jewish. However, they will affect how the person chooses to raise his or her children.

9. Many parents in interfaith relationships use Jewish communal institutions, especially educational institutions and programs, as surrogate parents. These institutions take the place of the adult partner who is not Jewish.

10. Compared to inmarried parents, intermarried parents take a greater interest in the Jewish education of their children, when they decide to provide such an education. Decisions that might be taken for granted by inmarried parents are carefully considered by intermarried parents.

Congregation Sukkat Shalom

Congregation Sukkat Shalom is in Wilmette, Illinois, a suburb on the shore of Lake Michigan north of Chicago. The congregation began in the spring of 1995, when fifteen families joined together. They had been meeting informally under the leadership of Rabbi Samuel Gordon, a pioneer in the field of outreach to those who had intermarried and, unlike most of his colleagues, one who was willing to officiate at interfaith weddings. Initially the group that would form Sukkat Shalom came together as a support group for intermarried couples with young children. Eventually they were joined by inmarried couples as well. However, almost all the members of the congregation are intimately involved with issues surrounding intermarriage. For example, some of the inmarried couples have adult children or adult grandchildren who have intermarried. Among the principles upon which they agreed and that the synagogue would follow was that families—adults and children—would learn together rather than separately, as is the case in most schools of religious instruction, so-called Hebrew or religious schools in North American synagogues.

One hundred people came together for High Holiday services in the fall during Sukkat Shalom's first year. The congregation's Family School, as it came to be known, began at the same time. Over the years, the synagogue met in various rented locations until purchasing its own building in 2012. Today the congregation numbers about 320 family units.

What makes the congregation unique in its affirmation of interfaith families is that its members "recognize and celebrate that we all come from diverse religious backgrounds but share an authentic quest for spiritual meaning and depth within the world of modern Judaism," according to Rabbi Gordon. Thus, when sacred texts are studied in the Family School, both Jewish and Christian interpretations are studied as a way of acknowledging the heritage of approximately half the adult members of the congregation. What is most important to the synagogue's leaders is the congregation's porosity and fluidity, especially when it comes to religious identification and community.

According to Gordon, a verse from Isaiah 56 provides the foundation for the synagogue's mission: "My house shall be a house of prayer for all people." Thus, he considers Sukkat Shalom "a sacred community for all people." Because of the diversity of its membership, Rabbi Gordon told me he believes "that anyone walking into our sanctuary for worship or seeking counseling from clergy or joining us for any reason must be seen not as an outsider or even a welcome visitor. They are part of our community. Sukkat Shalom, for that moment, must offer an authentic spiritual experience for everyone who is present."

Lessons Learned by Sukkat Shalom

1. Intermarriage is no longer a peripheral issue for the Jewish community. And those who have intermarried have moved into the mainstream of the North American Jewish community. Only some Jewish leaders see intermarriage as a problem. Congregations like Sukkat Shalom see intermarriage as an opportunity.

2. People who are intermarried do not seek support groups. They do not consider themselves any different from anyone else. They may seek education. Like most others, they seek community with meaning.

3. It is not unusual for the non-Jewish partner in an intermarriage to be the driving religious force in the family and thus become a cornerstone for the synagogue.

4. For adult partners in an intermarriage who come from a religious background other than Judaism, especially when those partners don't practice their faith of origin, the rabbi becomes their spiritual teacher, perhaps the only one they know. The boundaries that may be set up by the organized Jewish community to limit their participation in synagogue life seem irrelevant to them.

5. At Sukkat Shalom, family education, voluntary donations in place of dues, and serious text study all make sense to its members who come from religious backgrounds other than Judaism, because they are familiar with these practices from their religious upbringing.

Reflection and Discussion Questions for Synagogue Leaders

1. How can we more fully welcome interfaith families once we open our doors to them?

2. What needs to be changed in our synagogue culture to reflect the welcoming attitude that we want to promote?
3. How do we communicate the changes that we have made so that interfaith families feel more comfortable in our synagogue?

Intermarriage is not a new phenomenon, but its magnitude in our community at this point in Jewish history is what makes it so significant. Many Jewish leaders are afraid intermarriage might have a negative impact on the Jewish community. How synagogues—and the Jewish community—respond will determine how we can mitigate that impact and transform it into an opportunity for growth.

CHAPTER 5

Don't Forget the Boomers

Synagogue leaders assume that recruiting new members, particularly families with young children, is the only way to guarantee the future well-being of any synagogue. Given synagogue leaders' focus on this population, it is not surprising that many synagogue programming efforts are directed toward families with young children. Even holiday celebrations and the like—ostensibly for the entire synagogue community—are usually designed for the benefit of such family units. While I do not want to diminish the importance of engaging families with young children, synagogues often do so at the expense of the so-called boomer population, unintentionally alienating or at least not serving them. This is a dire mistake. That is why this chapter is titled as a warning to all Jewish communal leaders, especially planners: Don't forget the boomers—if you want to secure the future. As far as I am concerned, reaching boomers is a critical element in the strategic planning of nearly any synagogue.

Not surprising, boomers leave the synagogue—generally not to return—because the synagogue's focus on children no longer speaks to them. Boomers walk away from synagogue life when this child-centered focus fails to consider the configuration of their own boomer families, when the synagogue's repertoire of programs offers nothing that meets the specific needs of the boomer population. According to sociologist Herbert Gans, quoted by Jack Wertheimer, who teaches American Jewish history at the Jewish Theological Seminary of America, in *Commentary Magazine,* "They refrain from ethnic behavior that requires an arduous or time-consuming commitment either to a culture that must be practiced constantly, or to organizations that demand active membership." [1] Some boomers may not wait until they realize that the synagogue's focus on families with young children doesn't address their needs and leave following a life-cycle event such as a bar or bat mitzvah or when their kids finish the religious education program at the synagogue. This happens particularly with families whose initial motivation to join the synagogue was either religious education or *b'nai mitzvah* for their children. Membership in a synagogue implies certain obligations. With children out of the house and more freedom, many boomers decide that the synagogue just doesn't fit the lifestyle they are seeking.

Boomers are leaving the synagogue for additional reasons. The values that have shaped boomers periodically become evident in the ways boomers relate to the synagogue and the Jewish community. The current anti-affiliation of the boomer might be part of the anti-institution posture that began to develop during the Vietnam War and rose again during the 2008 banking crisis. They have rejected the lockstep curriculum that dominated the university (and other educational institutions) prior to the 1960s. Boomers have valued happiness over obligation and championed the American democratic spirit.

Who are the baby boomers? While the term has been used to refer to any group that indicates a population boom—an increase in the number of babies born—in any society, sociologists now generally employ the term to describe people who were born after World War II, specifically between the years 1946 and 1964. But the term *boomer* is also used to describe more than just a population bubble during this period. The term also refers to people who were in their teens and twenties in the 1960s and who rejected American (traditional) values that were accepted as status quo at the time. These values included loyalty, obligation, fidelity to family, and respect for government and authority, among others. Those values were turned upside down in the tumultuous sixties, when these boomers were developing their identity and core values. Evidence that these values were rejected includes expressions of free love (premarital sex); experimentation with illicit drugs such as marijuana; demonstrations against authority, particularly on college campuses and especially against the Vietnam War; and consumerism and general self-indulgence (that eventually generated the label the "me" generation). Beyond the Vietnam War, the various events that bound them as a group included the civil rights movement and the women's liberation movement, which were fueled by a commitment to democracy and egalitarianism. In general, the social segment of our society known as boomers—with Jews well represented—has become the most physically fit, well educated, financially successful, and influential of any generation in the United States to this point. Some sociologists and economists predict that subsequent generations—in the short term—will not be able to reach this exceptional level of well-being.

Throughout their lifetime, boomers have had an incredible impact on fashion and culture. Consider the Pepsi-Cola campaign in the 1960s when boomers turned eighteen and entered the prime eighteen to forty-nine cohort. Pepsi marketers coined the slogan "The drink of the new generation." Boomers made blue jeans a fashion statement and staple. But over time, marketers have misread what has been taking place. They have viewed boomers as a youth culture—which it was when boomers were young—but they have continued to emphasize youth even as boomers have aged. With the possible exception of hair coloring products and the like that are designed to keep boomers looking young, boomers seem to be rejecting that which is designed for young people. By focusing on youth to the near exclusion of other populations, the synagogue has made the same mistake as marketers. Synagogue 3000, a transdenominational project initiated about twenty years ago in an effort to help synagogues renew themselves, has changed its direction. Now it is primarily working to reach the elusive twenty- to thirty-year-olds in its Next Dor project (the name is a pun on the Hebrew word *dor*, "generation"). This is another example of a project that leaves the boomer population behind.

Boomers are not sitting quietly while the world ignores them. They are beginning to see start-ups, independent minyanim, study groups, and service learning programs—developed by and for the boomer generation. While these start-ups may be established to fulfill needs different from those that are inspiring the younger generation to engage Jewish life, the message to the synagogue is the same: You are not meeting our needs, so we're going to develop programs and institutions that meet our specific needs and interests—even if we must do so outside the synagogue. Boomers are the first generation raised to believe that their needs matter and can (and should) be fulfilled.

Given the world into which the boomers were born and that shaped their development and values, it is no surprise that the boomer generation is still not behaving like previous generations. It is true that the dress of boomers and even their voting patterns have become more conservative as boomers have aged. However, many of their behaviors are different from generations of the past. Their choices about retirement, particularly type of housing and locale, are among the most obvious differences. Members of this generation may downsize their homes or move into age-segregated housing (often euphemistically called an active adult lifestyle community). But they are not forsaking their local communities and moving to Florida and the Sun Belt the way their parents' generation did. Rather than seeking the sunshine, those who can afford a second home are more likely to purchase that second home wherever their adult children live, so that they can be close to grandchildren. Significant numbers of boomers are moving back to urban life. And we see some boomers moving into small university towns, where the cost of living is often reasonable and the cultural offerings are robust. Boomers are experiencing a variety of life transitions and the Jewish community has to be poised to respond to these life transitions.

Further, boomers are not actually retiring—that is, ceasing to work or be gainfully employed even if they have the financial wherewithal to stop working. Increasingly boomers opt to pursue a new career (sometimes called an encore career) rather than stay in the positions they have held throughout their middle years. Joseph Quinn, professor of economics at Boston College, calls these "bridge jobs." Loyalty to an employer no longer seems to be an important value. Yes, boomers are proud of what they have done or the comfortable life they built for their families. But now they want to make a difference in the world, to leave a lasting imprint. And some of those who worked in the for-profit sector during the majority of their adult lives are choosing to shape a second career in the nonprofit sector, particularly in the helping professions, often returning to school to be trained to do so.

This desire to be happy—and their discontent with the life they have led—has probably contributed to the increase in the divorce rate among boomers. They see the potential for thirty more productive years ahead of them and do not want to continue to live in an unhappy marriage. They want to make changes before it is indeed too late. Past generations did not often divorce once they reached the age at which boomers are divorcing, because these past generations saw the end of their lives approaching. Synagogues can position themselves to meet the needs that emerge from these psychosocial changes.

Impact of Boomer Behavior on the Synagogue

Unanticipated boomer behavior, that is, behaving in ways that are different from their parents, is particularly important to the synagogue community. The National Jewish Population Studies, sponsored by the Jewish Federations of North America (and its predecessors), consistently note that a majority of Jews are not members of synagogues. However, over their lifetime most Jews have been affiliated with synagogues, usually when they had children living at home. They left the synagogue when it no longer served the needs of their family. Synagogues resigned themselves to this reality and didn't attempt to make any major programmatic changes, because synagogues felt that the period of affiliation was sufficient to meet the needs of families, especially for life-cycle events, and the population boom sustained them, as did the expanding economy. However, people are no longer affiliating for the period (at least twenty years) anticipated by these population studies.

The primary way to engage the boomer generation in Jewish life is through programs that provide meaning to their lives, answering the perennial question, why am I here? One vehicle that has the potential to help boomers find the answers they are seeking to life's questions is education. Boomers are more likely than other generations, particularly families with young children, to have the discretionary funds and control over the time required for such study. But the study has to answer the big questions in life.

What are the big questions that boomers are asking themselves and the world around them? Are synagogues answering these questions? Will people be able to find answers in a synagogue worship experience? Here are a few of these questions:

- How can I leave this world a better place than it was when I entered it?

- What legacy of accomplishments will I leave when I die?
- How can I find work that makes a difference either in the world or in someone's life, work that improves the lives of people rather than just a job whose motive is profit alone?
- How can I develop and nurture a relationship with the Divine?

To be sure, adult Jewish education has to be different from education for children, in theory and in practice. One major difference between adult and children's education is that adults need to play a role in the shaping of their education, rather than letting someone else determine that direction for them.

There are some outstanding programs of adult study. For example, Context, Kolel: The Adult Centre for Liberal Jewish Learning, Me'ah, the Florence Melton School of Adult Jewish Learning, and the Wexner Heritage Program are all sophisticated programs of adult Jewish study. Only some of these programs, such as the Wexner Heritage Program, are independent of an institution or religious movement. Some, such as the Adult Centre for Liberal Jewish Learning, may have started as part of a religious organization but are now affiliated with another institution. A few, like the Skirball Center for Adult Jewish Learning in New York City, have been established by and housed at the synagogue, or contiguous to it, and yet are able to retain their independence. This is because the Skirball Center was established to benefit the community rather than its sponsoring institution. Among the Orthodox, there are synagogue-based study programs. These usually follow a traditional text-centered model, such as *daf yomi* (referring to the study of one page of Talmud per day). Some of these programs have established curricula. And while it is possible to address the questions of meaning posed by boomers in such a curricular approach, few are actually designed for that purpose.

How effective are these adult study programs in attracting boomers and meeting their needs? The Wexner Heritage
Program, one of the premier programs (funded by Leslie Wexner,
chairman of Limited Brands, and his wife, Abigail), was actually
designed as a leadership training program. It was never intended
to be primarily about adult study. Rather, its founders thought
that there was a dearth of Jewish knowledge among (primarily)
volunteer leaders and that these people could be better leaders if
they were better Jewishly equipped (read: more Jewishly educated
or literate). When the program began, it targeted people who
were poised to become leaders in the Jewish community. These
were coincidentally boomers. But as the program continued and
sought those who might become leaders, it targeted a younger
population and once again neglected the boomer population.
Thus, this program may not have been sufficient to meet the
needs of boomers.

The Florence Melton School for Adult Jewish Learning,
named for its original funder and visionary, is now a project of
the Hebrew University of Jerusalem. The formal two-year curriculum follows the course of Jewish history and thought and is
entirely cognitive. Its target population seems to be primarily
boomers, but it has no experiential element, and it certainly does
not attempt to answer life's big questions.

While classroom learning for its own sake may be sufficient for some boomers, it seems that a doing-while-learning
approach speaks to more of them. This is usually called
service learning, which combines study and volunteerism.
Unfortunately, while the number of service learning programs
is growing, many are misguided in their emphasis on reaching
young people rather than boomers. But this approach is critical
for engaging volunteers of all ages, according to David Elcott,
who teaches at New York University, and Stuart Himmelfarb,
well-known for his research background, especially among

college students. Together, they are the driving force behind B3/The Jewish Boomer Platform. B3 is a new initiative connecting baby boomers with the Jewish community by helping them identify second careers and providing options for volunteering, advocacy for programs that target boomers, and learning opportunities for boomers. Himmelfarb and Elcott observe that the approach reflects what boomers desire outside the Jewish community—service learning opportunities—and should therefore be replicated inside. If the Jewish community doesn't offer these opportunities, boomers will find them elsewhere. Service learning, thus, may be one significant answer to the question how to engage boomers, since it reflects the trend among boomers to participate in vocational or avocational work that makes a difference in the world.

But what's the goal of engaging the boomers? Is it merely to get them involved in (financially) supporting synagogues and Jewish communal institutions? I believe that engaging boomers has to be about more than attracting them for their potential financial support. Boomers are an underutilized resource; they can be recruited to participate in programs that are designed to improve our communities and make our world a better place in which to live. If programs are built on a foundation of Jewish values, then there is also the potential that such programs will nurture the spiritual lives of boomers. These programs can allow for a partnership among secular and Jewish organizations that may bring about a time Jewish religionists might call *mashiachzeit* (the Messianic era). According to the Torah, God created the world and directed humankind to become partners in completing that creation. If we are successful in reaching Jewish boomers and effect such positive outcomes in the community and the world, then as we harness the energy of the largest population among us, the effort could be one of the greatest transformations of the Jewish community in the twenty-first century.

Ten Things We Know about Boomers
and the Jewish Community

1. Boomers are the largest segment of the Jewish community. Thus, what the near Jewish future looks like may be the direct result of successfully reaching and engaging this population more than any other.
2. Boomers are not behaving like their parents and moving to the Sun Belt, and they are not abandoning their home communities. However, they may be rejecting familiar institutions that no longer speak to them.
3. Rather than retiring, boomers are often moving into encore professions. These include positions in Jewish communal work.
4. Boomers are looking for meaningful volunteer opportunities that the Jewish community can potentially provide or organize.
5. Boomers have more discretionary time and financial resources than the other three generations (millennials, generation X, and generation Y) who are currently in the work (and volunteer) environment. They will also inherit the largest transfer of wealth from one generation to another the United States has ever experienced.[2]
6. Some boomers are moving back into urban environments, living alongside the millennial generation.
7. Serious adult study that also answers life's big questions will attract a large segment of boomers.
8. Unlike families with young children, boomers are not looking to engage Judaism primarily through their children and grandchildren at holiday time. If they engage Judaism, they want to do on their own terms, as adults.
9. Boomers will experience more life changes and transitions than previously experienced in their lives, and the Jewish community has to be prepared to guide them—and support them—during these transitions.

10. Boomers are not seeking additional obligations. They are seeking things to do that will enhance their lives and through which they can feel a direct benefit as a result of participation.

The Klene Up Krewe

While boomer programming is gaining some traction in secular circles, especially in government-sponsored programs, boomer programs in the Jewish community have yet to be fully defined. Because boomers don't follow familiar paths, boomer programs have a lot of room to grow and succeed. These programs are multilayered and continuing to evolve. But it is clear that serious hands-on volunteer activity is one sure way to engage a large segment of boomers, particularly those who are looking to make a transition from the work they have been doing for the majority of their lives to meaningful volunteer engagement. Much of this engagement is episodic. We have few examples of successful boomer engagement programs from which we can draw inferences about how to program well for this population and grow the local congregation. Given that limitation, consider the Klene Up Krewe project described in this section as a program pilot.

Enter Larry Weiss and David Goodman. Both Weiss and Goodman, volunteer community leaders, were emotionally overwhelmed by the devastation caused by Hurricane Katrina in New Orleans, Louisiana, in 2005 and by the vast number of people—particularly those already impoverished—who had lost their homes. They had both attended Tulane University and remembered the city fondly. What troubled them most was not the destruction caused by the natural disaster. Rather, the failed human response to that disaster is what motivated them to act.

Because Weiss and Goodman understood that associating with a Jewish communal organization could give them legitimacy and access, they approached the Jewish Federation of Northern New Jersey for sponsorship. The federation could also provide them with up-to-date information about projects in New Orleans that needed assistance. The federation agreed, permitting its staff member, Stuart Himmelfarb, to work with Weiss and Goodman and assemble a group that would go to New Orleans to provide whatever help was needed. Otherwise, the federation stayed out of the way. While some in federation leaders wanted to see a return on their investment, the group was supported by the federation— no strings attached. Thus, the Klene Up Krewe was born.

The first trip to New Orleans in September 2006 attracted seventeen people, all adults, and all somehow friends of Weiss, Goodman, and Himmelfarb. They worked with a local project to build homes. This trip included a visit to the synagogue in Biloxi, Mississippi, which was also hit by the same storm that devastated New Orleans. The leaders of this first cohort knew that they were feeling their way; the group didn't know what they would actually encounter. Thus, they were hesitant to expand the group or actively solicit participants. Since that first trip, however, the founders of the program have gathered groups to go to New Orleans and build homes two to three times a year, often over a holiday weekend. As part of their efforts, they have raised funds for Katrina relief through the federation and have earmarked some of the funds for rebuilding the synagogue they had visited in Mississippi.

Unlike the participants in other Jewish communal programs, these volunteers are neither carrying out the work they undertake as part of their "day job" nor doing busy work. Volunteers insist, "I don't want to just show up. I want to dig in and roll up my sleeves." Their eagerness to contribute significantly is especially evident when they arrive for what is called a twenty-four-hour build (of a house). For all who participated there were tangible results. They could see in concrete terms the Jewish value of repairing the world.

Lessons Learned by the Klene Up Krewe

1. Earlier experiences in a program for boomers will help determine what later activities to include as the program or project evolves.
2. Boomers seek meaningful volunteer activities and eschew meaningless activities that have been the hallmark of some volunteer programs in the past.
3. When boomers volunteer, they don't want to do things they would normally do, either as part of their profession or even around their own homes.
4. Jewish boomers see such volunteer activities as an extension or expression of Jewish values.
5. Intergenerational activities can enhance the experience, especially when opportunities for reciprocal mentorship present themselves.

Reflection and Discussion Questions for Synagogue Leaders

1. What will it take to persuade synagogue leadership that to ensure the sustainability of our institution, reaching boomers is as important as reaching families with young children?
2. Should programs for boomers be multigenerational? If so, then what programs can reach multiple generations at the same time?
3. What volunteer activities need to be developed that can enhance the mission of the institution and provide meaningful experiences for boomers at the same time?

Boomers represent a strong and forceful generation. By successfully reaching and engaging boomers, we have the opportunity to transform Jewish communal life once again.

CHAPTER 6

The Dream of Israel

This book is about the future of the Jewish community. It is also about the survival of the synagogue. There is among Jewish leaders a great deal of discussion about whether the contemporary Jewish community can survive without a deep and abiding connection to the modern state of Israel. This is especially important at a time when interest in Israel from large numbers of American Jews is waning, particularly among the younger population and intermarried families. For most Jews in North America, Israel and the Jewish community have been synonymous. The general public often sees them the same way. In fact, many synagogues and Jewish communal institutions rely heavily on Israel to jumpstart or nurture Jewish identity. That's why many communal institutions have regularly scheduled trips—often called missions—to Israel. They want to bring people into a firsthand encounter with the land of Jewish ancestry, and they think that passion for Israel, the kind such trips foster, will lead to participants' renewed interest in the sponsoring institution.

For Jewish communal institutions to effectively harness Israel in the process of building support for their institutions, these institutions must first help the individual establish a relationship with Israel. This is often accomplished by fostering pride in what Israel does, particularly its accomplishments. Israel is a mainstay in religious school and Jewish day school curricula and features prominently in synagogue and communal programming. Thus, there can be no fruitful discussion about the future of the North American Jewish community and the future of the synagogue without a discussion about Israel. However, this chapter is not about the history of the state of Israel, how it came into being, or the politics that govern the daily life of its citizens. Nor is it about the Palestinian conflict or Israel's interactions with its neighboring states. Rather, this chapter is about the role that Israel plays in determining the future shape of the North American Jewish community, in fostering the identity of its members, and in helping to secure the future of the synagogue.

Israel has always had a pivotal place in Jewish religion and culture. Jerusalem was the center of the temple cult after the Hebrews inhabited the land following the exodus from Egypt, although religious centers were located throughout the entire land. After the Jews' historical exile from Israel in 586–538 BCE, the people's longing to return was woven into Jewish liturgy, as evidenced in the prayer book. Few Jewish rituals or ceremonies do not contain a reference to Israel. And once the modern nation state was born, Israel became an indispensable partner with the organized North American Jewish community in developing Jewish identity. The importance of this role may seem ironic to some, since Israel was born as a secular state and most of its citizens are secular rather than religious—although being a secular Jew in Israel is different from being a secular Jew in the United States.

There is a significant disconnect between most Israelis and synagogues in Israel. Many will argue that it is because the majority of Israelis are secular and not interested in Israeli synagogues, which are mostly Orthodox. But this is an oversimplification of the issue. Most Israelis would not be considered secular if they were viewed through the lens of American religious practice. They observe the Israeli version of civil religion, that is, national holidays and civic events. But *civil* religion in Israel encompasses what American Jews might call *cultural* Judaism, a legitimate expression of Judaism, to be sure. Civil Judaism is practiced in the public sphere and is often devoid of any theological connection. Rather, it represents the folk more than anything else, and the connection of that folk to their past. That most Israelis practice a civil form of Jewish religion is particularly evident on the holidays, which are primarily though not exclusively observed inside the synagogue in North America and outside the synagogue in Israel. Israelis do mark these observances, just not according to historic Jewish religious standards. And these traditional religious standards are the measures by which American synagogues have incorrectly defined Israel and the Israeli as secular. By describing Israel and Israelis as secular, that is, nonreligious, American Jewish communal leaders are also making a judgment about the increasing number of those who may want to observe Jewish holidays in North America the same way that many Israelis do in Israel—outside the synagogue.

Perhaps it is because most North American Jews are not affiliated with synagogues and do not participate in most religious rituals (except for the High Holidays, Passover, and Hanukkah) that Jewish community leaders are not concerned that most Israelis are secular. Nevertheless, Israel has played a significant role in the development of Jewish identity among North American Jews. It must also be said that American Jews have played an important role in providing financial support for the state, as well as political support through the U.S. government. While Israel's part in the development of positive Jewish identity—what might be called Jewish pride—has been evident since 1948 (associated with the establishment of the modern state and the war that followed), it has been particularly manifest in North America since the Six Day War of 1967. The Jewish pride that ensued as a result of the unusual performance by Israel's armed forces in 1967 provoked many Jews in North America to express their Jewish identity outside the walls of Jewish communal institutions, something that many had previously been afraid to do. More traditional Jewish men were willing to wear their *kipot* (traditional skullcaps) out in the open, without the familiar camouflage provided by baseball caps. Similarly, secular Jews began to wear *kipot* as a sign of their Jewish identity, irrespective of their religious practices. Covering their heads with a *kipah* (singular of *kipot*) was their statement of Jewish pride, which found its roots in Israel.

This post–Six Day War period also saw an increase in the number of Hebrew language classes offered in synagogues in the United States, courses that went far beyond "reading Hebrew," especially in the prayer book (siddur), which had previously been de rigueur. Immersive Hebrew programs following the Israeli *ulpan* style of *Ivrit b'Ivrit* (Hebrew in Hebrew) instruction became much more normative, although this format has decreased in popularity in the United States in more recent years. Conversational Hebrew instruction, although not directly relevant to the learning of prayer-book Hebrew, has eclipsed any other type of Hebrew class in the United States. With the onset of sophisticated Internet technology, such Hebrew programs are being offered directly from Israel, the most popular one simply called "Hebrew On-Line."

Synagogue trips to Israel, particularly in the so-called mission format, also increased after the Six Day War. These were often community-wide trips whose ostensible purpose was to expose people to all that is Israel, but whose hidden agenda was to pull at the heartstrings of participants so that they would be motivated to increase their donations to the nascent state through their local Jewish Federation's financial campaign, a portion of which goes to support social service programs in Israel. These missions to Israel afforded participants the opportunity to encounter first-hand the land and its people. The trips provided participants with profound—sometimes life-changing—emotional experiences, but they generally did not provide trip participants with a real encounter with Israel. These trips failed to show them the real Israel, warts and all. Thus, the Israel they experienced didn't seem real, and it certainly was not the Israel that they read about in daily newspapers or heard about on the evening news. This narrow encounter with the real Israel was compounded by religious school instruction in the United States, where textbooks used by children in the synagogue showed a similarly unrealistic portrait of Israel. So children were raised with an image of Israel to which it was difficult for them to relate. And besides further fundraising, the local synagogue seldom followed up to connect trip participants to the synagogue. This follow-up is indispensable if we really want to use Israel effectively to build Jewish identity and also see why Israel contains part of the answer to the question, why be Jewish? (see chapter 7). It's time that synagogues develop trips to Israel that help nurture the Jewish soul with an eye toward strengthening individuals' connections to their local synagogues and communities.

I believe that trips can be designed to nurture Jewish identity if they reflect the particular interests of participants. Like other programs sponsored by the synagogue, Israel trips have to reflect the needs of the individual rather than the needs of the sponsoring institution. And then the synagogue has to help the person make the connection between what he or she experiences in Israel and the Jewish-rooted behavior promoted by the synagogue, such as Hebrew language study.

In using trips to Israel to nurture Jewish identity, one challenge is, after such journeys, to build paths that lead participants from their trip into engagement with the synagogue. Without a map showing the connections, people will not know what direction to take. There are some claims to the contrary, however. Birthright Israel (which offers free nine-day trips to Israel for college students and twentysomethings) presents data that suggest the program motivates travelers to participate in synagogue life as the primary Jewish communal institution following their

return from Israel. And indeed, Birthright Israel has established
a new benchmark or gold standard for Israel trips: they are free
and reach large numbers of their target population. As a result,
those who otherwise may have taken a trip sponsored by another
organization—especially teenagers—now frequently wait until
they are eligible for the *free* Birthright trips. Although other trips
may be longer in duration and provide participants with greater
exposure to Israel and its citizens, the fact that the Birthright trips
are free seems to be sufficient motivation for people to forego
taking high school trips to Israel sponsored by numerous Jewish
youth groups. And according to research conducted on Birthright
Israel participants, their short trip can be transformative. But
Birthright Israel trips are a diminishing asset. If we want these
trips to be effective vehicles for connecting young Jews with
the organized Jewish community and the synagogue, then it is
important for synagogues to build a clear route from these trips
into synagogue life as soon as people return from their trips.
Participating in a trip will not in itself naturally take them into
the synagogue.

Trips to Israel yield connections of various kinds. Political
advocacy and philanthropy have been the primary vehicles that
the organized Jewish community, especially synagogues, has
employed to motivate people to maintain ties with Israel. Even if
they were once sufficient motivators, however, political advocacy
and philanthropy don't work any longer to reach and engage the
majority of American Jews. The Jewish Federation system in
North America, for example, was built through this approach of
engaging people through political advocacy and philanthropy,
but it is losing a great deal of its reach as the number of its do-
nors is shrinking. As an alternative tactic, Martin Raffel, senior
vice president of the Jewish Council for Public Affairs, recom-
mends an approach he calls "shared interests and shared values."
He argues that people are attracted to issues and institutions
because they share interests and values with those institutions.

Raffel believes that if the North American Jewish community can demonstrate to the potential participants it wants to attract and engage that they share specific interests and values with Israel, then these American Jews will be interested in interacting with Israel by supporting it, politically and financially, and by visiting it. As a result, he argues, the Jewish identity of these American Jews can be ignited, nurtured, and strengthened. Raffel also suggests that this model of identifying and promoting shared interests and values in Israel can be the model around which synagogues attract people to the synagogue.

There are many organizations—including United Synagogue Youth (USY), who are youth associated with the Conservative Jewish religious movement—whose trips predate Birthright Israel trips. Among other things, these USY trips promote religious observances and practices that reflect the Conservative movement, even if they do not always reflect the level of religious observance of participants' families. After a summer of such engagement and enhanced religious observance, young people often come home and find their parents do not support such practices. Since the synagogue does not intervene, the interest of these young people and the discipline of religious practice they have established may diminish over time. While it may be hard to recruit participants to USY trips—or any other trips to Israel—once young people do participate, synagogues have to do more to integrate them back into the life of the synagogue. These institutions need to help congregants prepare for their children's return from Israel trips by accommodating their newly discovered religious practices.

When I went to Israel for the first time, I was sixteen years old. I was armed only with images of Israel I had absorbed from the religious school textbooks of my childhood. These included traditional folk dancing in the streets, eighteenth-century Polish religious garb, and a pioneering spirit that animated its citizenry. To be sure, I encountered some of these images, especially since my first encounter with the land of Israel took place more than forty years ago. Much has changed since that time. But many of these folk-dancing, minimalist, pioneer images, which are imprinted on the individual and shaped by controlled trips to Israel, have not changed at all. So people who go to Israel today often see the same staged stereotypes I saw years ago. Instead, synagogues have to help individuals grapple with the reality of Israel—particularly the nation's struggle to become a modern state.

There are synagogue-based rabbis who are afraid to speak about Israel, concerned that their political position may be too critical of Israel's domestic policy or too affirming of the rights of the Palestinians, politically charged issues and positions that may be to the left of congregants. These rabbis fear that such speaking out may place their employment at risk. But my own teacher, Rabbi Samuel Sandmel, of blessed memory, once taught me that I should take actions that place my rabbinate at risk every day. And while I don't encourage colleagues to do things intentionally to lose their jobs, I do want them to take principled stands about significant issues, including those relevant to Israel, such as settlement expansion, women's rights to pray at the Kotel (remaining Western Wall of the ancient temple courtyard), and the rights of Palestinians—irrespective of where on the political spectrum they stand.

One way the synagogue can renew itself—and attract people to it, especially those who might be interested in exploring their relationship to Israel—is by becoming a safe space for civil discourse in the United States with regard to Israel, a place where these conversations can occur without criticism or judgment. Often, Israel education is merely a euphemism for Israel advocacy. By not providing objective education about Israel so that people can draw their own conclusions about Israel's domestic issues, those who are struggling over the various issues confronting Israel often become disenchanted and disinterested in Israel and the Jewish community, which they see as synonymous. Making the synagogue a safe space for such conversations will strengthen it in the community. And if the synagogue can become such as safe space, it has the potential to strengthen the ties between those who participate in the dialogue about Israel and the nation of Israel itself. By becoming a safe space for such dialogue, the synagogue opens up the possibility that it can become a safe space for dialogue about other issues and thereby enlarge the role it plays for people who might potentially engage in the synagogue. This will help restore the synagogue to a place of prominence in North America.

Even if synagogues become safe spaces for dialogue, adopting such practices may be insufficient for synagogues as they consider their role regarding Israel and the Jewish community. Rabbis, as spiritual leaders, have to become spiritual guides for the individual's encounter with Israel in word, deed, and thought. In so doing, these rabbis can give new meaning to the role Israel plays in shaping the Jewish identity of the individual.

Things Synagogues Can Do to Engage People through Israel

Using the Calendar

- Tu Bishevat and Earth Day: Host programs focused on environmentalism. For example, highlight Israeli technology in irrigation, reforestation, and solar energy.
- Yom Hazikaron: Form alliances with American veterans groups and military groups focused on security.
- Yom Ha'atzmaut: Partner with democracy advocacy groups and employ the methods of outreach at parades and celebrations that reach tens of thousands.
- Hanukkah and Passover: Make connections with these most celebrated Jewish holidays in North America, both

of which commemorate events that happened in (or going into) Israel.

COLLABORATIVE PROGRAMMING

- Serve Israeli food at outdoor festivals or food festivals.
- Offer Israeli music in the midst of musical programs.
- Teach Israeli dance during dance festivals.
- Establish Israeli themes at conferences, such as Israeli feminism at feminist conferences.
- Teach *krav maga* to kids who may already be involved or interested in martial arts or self-defense and participating in self-image building; for example, programs like D.A.R.E.
- Promote tie-ins to current events, such as the film *Munich* or concerns over Iran.

LOCATIONS TO CONSIDER

- Plan programs in street fairs. Include Israeli musical performances and Israeli food. Make sure that the booth is activity-based and represents Israeli culture.
- Stage Israeli plays at local (live) theaters and make sure that Israeli films are included in secular and Jewish film festivals.
- Place events in parks, stadiums, and concert halls.
- Also plan programs in malls, shopping plazas, and supermarkets, because that is where people are.

The Shalom Hartman Institute

The Shalom Hartman Institute is a pluralistic Orthodox institution founded by the late Rabbi David Hartman in

1976 in memory of his father and now led by his son Rabbi Donniel Hartman. David Hartman, an Orthodox rabbi, philosopher, and theologian, immigrated to Israel in 1971 following his tenure at Congregation Tiferet Beit David Jerusalem in Montreal. The iEngage Project was established by the institute to change the narrative about Israel from post-Holocaust survivalism—what the younger Hartman calls a "death narrative"— particularly among world Jews who are economically, politically, and culturally successful and with whom such a narrative no longer resonates. While the institute affirms the dangers that Israel faces, it acknowledges its military prowess as well.

The project helps participants understand how Israel can enhance their own Jewish identity and bring meaning to people's lives while helping them imagine a vision for Israel that exhibits the highest of Jewish moral standards. The program is conducted by a group of scholars led by Tal Becker through a free, monthly, live, Internet-based lecture series. The sessions are archived for those unable to attend the live sessions. Hartman is trying to forge what he calls a "new covenant" between Israel and world Jewry that is symbiotic rather than one directional.

Approximately 130 congregations are using the Engaging Israel DVD series, with a total of approximately 2,600 participants. About 35 congregations are teaching the Peoplehood DVD series, with a total of approximately 350 participants. In some synagogues, the Engaging Israel series is presented on a video feed from Israel and then is facilitated by local rabbis.

LESSONS LEARNED BY THE SHALOM HARTMAN INSTITUTE

1. While bringing people to Israel may be the best way to engage folks with Israel, it is not always realistic.
2. Deeper learning is fostered more in group rather than in individual sessions, but offering individuals the option of

participating makes it possible to serve a larger number of people, especially in remote locations.

3. People are looking for ways to develop a new narrative about Israel that reflects the reality of their personal Jewish experiences.

4. Introducing Israel in an educational context helps neutralize the potential politicization of Israel dialogue.

5. Pluralism is a value in the liberal Jewish community much more than in the Orthodox community, particularly regarding Israel.

Reflection and Discussion Questions for Synagogue Leaders

1. How does a relationship with Israel foster Jewish identity?
2. How can we reach outside the synagogue in order to engage the broader community in dialogue about Israel?
3. How can we translate Israel engagement into synagogue engagement?

Israel remains a critical item on the agenda of the North American Jewish community. Much of the concern has been about Israel's security. While this concern is real, the community also has to look beyond security concerns and harness Israel to help shape American Jewish identity. This approach to nurturing Jewish identity will require Jewish scholars and teachers to develop a new narrative and a new symbiotic partnership between Israel and the North American Jewish community.

Chapter 7

Why Be Jewish?

If one reviews the various educational offerings of Jewish communal institutions from the past twenty-five years, one can easily deduce what central question is being answered by the array of programs being offered. The educational question during that period, especially the era that shaped the boomer generation, was, what skills do I need to do "Jewish"? As a result, most educational programs focused specifically on the "how to" of Jewish life. I even coauthored with my colleague Rabbi Ron Isaacs a very well-received book called *The Complete How-To Handbook for Jewish Living*.

In the language of a popular educational theory of the 1960s called confluent education, the major question asked by educators was not related to cognition or intellect or affect or emotion. Rather, educators were focused primarily—if not exclusively—on psychosocial and motor skills. They were asking, what are the skills needed to do a particular act, primarily a ritual act, correctly? Borrowing the language of the leading American educator of the early twentieth century, John Dewey, who predated the school of confluent educational theory by sixty or more years, the question could be phrased, what are the skills one needs to know to function as a full-fledged citizen in the community? Jewish leaders believed that a lack of cultural literacy—and particularly the skills associated with it—was keeping people out of the synagogue and out of the Jewish community, in general. As a result, went the logic of such thinking, skill-focused education would be all that was needed to engage the unengaged and bring people into the synagogue and other Jewish communal institutions.

I believe that an answer to the question, what skills do I need to become a functioning Jew? is no longer what people are seeking. In this current generation, the question that seems to trump all others is, why be Jewish at all? In particular, synagogue leaders have to be willing to answer the question, why be Jewish in this particular institutional environment? In other words, people want to know how their lives will be made better. How will they personally benefit from their participation? How will the lives of their families be positively influenced by participation in this group? And finally, what are the costs and benefits of participation? Answers to these questions are particularly important for parents in an intermarried family who have to make a choice about the religion in which to raise their children. Eliyahu Stern, now assistant professor of Modern Jewish Intellectual and Cultural History at Yale University, implemented one of the early "Why Be Jewish?" conferences for the Samuel Bronfman Foundation. He put the challenge to the community's professionals and volunteer leaders this way: "Most importantly, we need to convey that Judaism adds a palpable higher value to our life experience. A strong and enduring Judaism must be able to provide answers, supply meaning and address issues that affect the way we live."[1]

I have spoken to some synagogue and Jewish communal leaders who do not see their responsibility as providing others with a motivation or reason to be Jewish or to engage Jewishly. Some of these leaders see even characterizing the notion of being Jewish as something that can benefit the individual as rather narcissistic. Why, they ask, should the Jewish community be there to serve the individual member? Instead of adopting language that reflects how the synagogue should benefit the individual, these naysayers prefer the language of obligation, the language common to most Jewish communal institutions. They want those who participate in synagogue life to ask, what are *my* obligations to the community? How can my participation benefit it? The tension between obligation and benefit reflects the debate sometimes provoked by the oft-quoted refrain of President John F. Kennedy, who challenged the American public, "Ask not what your country can do for you. Ask what you can do for your country." Perhaps this was a correct posture for an American president in the 1960s, but it is not the relevant question in the early decades of the twenty-first century for the majority of the Jewish community. The language of obligation will generally not entice individuals to join the community or participate in it. Rather, it might more likely turn people off and push them in another direction completely.

People on the liberal end of the Jewish religious spectrum generally shy away from the question, why be Jewish? They are afraid that asking the question may not be politically correct. The answer would certainly not be politically correct if it places Judaism in a position superior to another faith group. Even the possibility of placing one religion over another is particularly challenging for interfaith families, since embracing one religion may be seen as rejecting another. And if we look at the comparative benefits of two religions from the perspective of children in an interfaith family, embracing one religion may be misinterpreted as rejecting the other parent. But however difficult it may be to consider the benefits of participating in Jewish life, we have to grapple with this question if synagogues, as representatives of the Jewish religion, are going to argue that Judaism contains ideas and values to which people want to relate and call their own. Perhaps the notion of struggling over ideas is one reason why the biblical etymology for the name Israel (following Jacob's struggle with the angel, as recounted in the book of Genesis) is indeed "struggling with the Divine." Nothing of Judaism or Jewish belief came easily for our ancestors. Why should we expect it to come easily for us?

Because Jewish civilization is associated with Jewish people and culture and not just the Jewish religion, there are those, including the millennial generation, who will reject the question, why be Jewish? as one that reflects an insular and limiting tribalism. Perhaps tribalism can be newly understood not as limited to a group of people but in relationship to a set of ideas (in this case, Jewish ideas) and the people who hold them. This kind of tribalism might connect individual Jews to Jewish people without restricting us. This idea was explored in chapter 3 as Jewish ideas enter the marketplace of ideas without Jewish communal institutions connected to them. As readers will recall, promoting Judaism in the marketplace of ideas means making Jewish ideas available to anyone, Jews and non-Jews alike. But why should people want to take on the foundational ideas of Judaism, whether they are born Jewish or are simply interested in what Judaism has to offer? And for those who were not born as Jews, why voluntarily enter into a covenantal relationship with the Divine? (These questions will be answered below.) By including the covenant with God as a foundational idea in Judaism, the covenantal relationship places Jewish religion at the center of Jewish civilization and culture. So being Jewish is about ideas and the people who hold these ideas rather than about the people themselves irrespective of the ideas to which they lay claim.

Some people would argue that the question, why be Jewish? can perhaps be answered in as many ways as there are Jewish people. While there is some truth to that, communal leaders also have to ask, why belong to Jewish communal institutions? I think some ideas about Judaism are universally accepted, forming what some might even refer to as *essential Judaism*. Rabbi Yitz Greenberg, named these ideas *common Judaism*, referring to those elements that all Jewish religious denominations have in common. Ellis Rivkin, who taught Jewish history at Hebrew Union College–Jewish Institute of Religion, went even further. He boiled Judaism down to one concept, which he called *the unity principle*. It refers both to God's unity (monotheism) and to the unity of the Jewish people, who were brought into relationship with God at the defining moment of the Sinaitic experience, however that is to be understood.

When we discuss the essential concepts of Judaism, it is better to do so from a personal perspective, rather than approaching them as abstract concepts that are reserved for the classroom. In this way, essential Judaism is an expression of the self rather than the affirmation of the ideas of others. I believe that Judaism has to speak to the individual if it is to have meaning for individual lives. This approach transcends the limited definition of tribalism, because ideas are open to anyone who wants to claim them as his or her own.

It is true that all of us, even those of us who have Jewish parents, are Jews by choice. I *choose* to be Jewish and live an observant life, within the organized Jewish community. This is what makes me a Jew-by-choice. Still, as challenging and irascible they may often be, I love the Jewish people. The journey of the Jewish people through history courses through my blood. The memory of this journey is imprinted on my psyche. I believe that Judaism provides me with a path for personal redemption and the tools to help redeem the world as well. Personal redemption comes from living "the good life," and when I fail, Judaism guides me on the path of return. In so doing, Judaism affords me the opportunity to develop an intensely personal relationship with the Divine and elevate the routine of everyday living into the sacred. Jewish rituals ground me and provide me a rudder in the turbulent waters of daily living, while at the same time directing me in the work of repairing the world (what is called in Hebrew *tikkun olam*). This repair work takes us all in the direction of a time when the world will be more perfect, a time understood in Judaism as messianic living.

This is my personal answer to the question, why be Jewish? Others need to find the way to answer to the question for themselves, and synagogues have to assist in the process. Judaism provides me with a framework for living, so that I can continue to do the work of creation that was started when the world was conceived. Why am I Jewish? In short, because its values speak to me, sustain me, and elevate me so that I might soar heavenward. Rabbi David Wolpe, spiritual leader of Sinai Temple in Los Angeles, California, answers the question, why be Jewish? in his own way. Here is what he wrote:

> Because Judaism can teach us how to deepen our lives, to improve the world, to join with others who have the same lofty aims. Judaism can teach us spiritual and moral mindfulness, a way of living in this world that promotes joy inside of us and also encourages ethical action. But finally, the answer to why be Jewish must reside in the mystery of each seeking soul, trying to find its place with others and with God.[2]

Rabbi Wolpe identifies what he sees as the difficulty for the individual in answering the why be Jewish question. That person must confront the ideas of Judaism and then determine whether those ideas resonate with him or her. Synagogue leaders must in turn determine what would motivate individuals to engage their institution as representative of those Jewish ideas and ideals.

Another colleague, Rabbi Brant Rosen, takes a different perspective on the why be Jewish question:

> Because it gives us the opportunity to participate in this remarkable and still fairly unprecedented project. And I'll say it again: this global peoplehood that transcends national boundaries, that makes room for cultural diversity, and that affirms a dynamic, evolving religious

vision. I would go even further and say that this model has a great deal to offer in this particular age—as we witness an increasingly globalized post-ethnic, post-national world. Why be Jewish? Because we model a spiritual peoplehood that values struggle and debate, that is not afraid to take God to task, that seeks to challenge the icons of the status quo, particularly—as the prophets so eloquently teach us—the icons of the powerful and the privileged.[3]

Martin Raffel, senior vice president of the Jewish Council for Public Affairs, cautions us that when answering the why be Jewish question, it is not helpful to answer it in the form of a response to anti-Semitism, the Holocaust, or anti-Israel sentiment. Jewish identity should be framed as a positive statement, a positive influence on one's life. To be Jewish is to lay claim to a rich, three-thousand-year-old, life-affirming civilization with values that can provide meaning and direction for one's personal life values; that, if acted upon, can improve the quality of life for everyone on our planet; and that can help repair this fractured world. Being Jewish today also means claiming a relationship to a national sovereign Jewish entity, the domestic and foreign policies of which can reflect those values and traditions.

Ten Answers to the Question, Why Be Jewish?

I spend a lot of time consulting with synagogues and helping them to answer the question, why be Jewish? Here is my personal list. It is also the list I offer institutions in order to begin the process of finding the answer for themselves.

1. As a Jew, the collective story of the Jewish people becomes my personal story. My own life's story contributes to the collective memory of the Jewish people. Jewish history is not the recording of events over time. Rather, the historical narrative of the Jewish people evolves toward a specific

goal—the messianic period—as the Jewish people move forward in history. By claiming a role in the unfolding of Jewish history, I am able to participate in the messianic period as well.

2. The doing of mitzvot brings me closer to the Divine. In the refracted Divine light, I am able to see myself more clearly.

3. The emphasis on deed over creed encourages the individual (irrespective of personal belief or doubts of faith) to help build a better world through acts of social justice (*tikkun olam*, repair of the world) and provides the individual with a variety of opportunities to do so. Doing these good deeds, which emerge from a foundation of positive Jewish values, brings me closer to others and to humanity.

4. The affirmation of one God is the unity principle that is the foundation of Jewish faith. Judaism encourages questioning and debate. Faith comes through struggle. The result of this struggle helps to define Jewish theology and my personal relationship to this one God and faith in God.

5. The Jewish community provides support to the individual (and family) during life's liminal moments, including those when we are overwhelmed by joy and those when we are deeply saddened.

6. Judaism transforms daily routine (the long haul of life) into sacred moments and sacred opportunities, especially through ritual, helping to moor us in what is sometimes an anchorless world.

7. Judaism emphasizes lifelong educational growth of all kinds. Jewish education helps us navigate the world morally. (The Talmud requires parents to teach their children "how to swim.") Judaism also provides a framework for teaching children their moral responsibility to the world.

8. The spiritual disciplines of Judaism—including daily prayer, the study of sacred texts, dietary standards, and Shabbat—elevate the soul.

9. Judaism fosters Jewish ethnicity, which connects Jews with one another, transcending any geographic border or time and space. As a Jew, I am never alone.

10. Jews have a home in Israel. Its capital, Jerusalem, is the center of the Jewish spiritual world where, according to rabbinic teaching, heaven and earth touch. As a Jew, that is my place, my home.

Rabbi Sharon Brous and Ikar

Rabbi Sharon Brous, the charismatic leader of Ikar, an alternative synagogue community in Los Angeles, understands the need to answer the question, why be Jewish? and to demonstrate institutionally the answer. According to Brous:

> To be Jewish today is to be animated by both gratitude and unrest, by humility and audacity. It is to recognize the utter magnificence of the world, the miracle of human life and human connection, the possibility of love and the abundance of life's blessings. And it is, at the same time, to feel the exodus from Egypt—the journey from slavery to freedom, from degradation to dignity—in our guts. It is to refuse to accept a world saturated with injustice, oppression and human suffering, and to become agents of social change whose fiercest weapons are love, faith and holy chutzpah.[4]

And so, since the founding of Ikar in 2004 by Brous and Melissa Balaban, the synagogue's executive director, Ikar has become a place for those searching for "a different kind of Jewish experience" and a "passion for social justice."[5]

Ikar provides participants with progressive, nondenominational Judaism in the same spirit as Congregation B'nai Jeshurun and Kehillat Hadar, both in New York City. Ikar's signature style of worship is free-form, which includes an intense drum circle. Deeply committed to its social engagement programs, Ikar has, for example, worked with an interfaith coalition to bring about changes in the LAPD's towing and impound policies, which targeted immigrants.

Today, the synagogue's roster includes more than five hundred family units (mostly families of young adults), and more than sixty children are enrolled in its preschool program. As they consider erecting a building to house this new approach to Jewish engagement, they say they intend to build "a dynamic center of Jewish engagement," a new style of Jewish community center. To do this, they plan to update the Jewish center model conceived by Rabbi Mordecai Kaplan almost a century ago and to include "sacred space, open art studio space, a music lab, a library/beit midrash/beit café, outdoor gathering and garden space [and] a learning center (for children and adults)."[6] As in any other institution, its leaders are concerned about how to pay for it all. But they believe that the center will help people answer the question, why be Jewish? by offering an exciting array of programs and services that meet the needs of the target population Ikar has already begun to attract.

Lessons Learned by Rabbi Brous and Ikar

1. According to Rabbi Brous, we have to be prepared to question the assumptions around every holiday and every program. We have to constantly ask ourselves: What is the essence of this event, and how can we make this essence manifest through our programs and holiday events?
2. For any program to be inspirational for participants, its leaders have to be inspired as well. For a program to

answer, why be Jewish? its leaders have to answer the question before they can help program participants do so.

3. As an alternative structure begins to look more like a traditional institution, extra care has to be taken to maintain its intimacy and responsiveness to the needs of participants.

4. Institutions have to be ready to capture people who seek the services that the institution provides.

5. The synagogue-as-center model still has potential to reach a broad range of those who are unaffiliated with the organized Jewish community or unengaged by it if the synagogue-as-center can answer the why be Jewish question.

Reflection and Discussion Questions for Synagogue Leaders

1. Can a community like Ikar be created outside of large Jewish communities such as Los Angeles? What adjustments to the model would need to be made in smaller communities?

2. Are such communities dependent on charismatic spiritual leaders? If so, then how do institutions find and nurture such leaders?

3. How will such an institution avoid the challenges of maintaining a physical plant whose overhead is overwhelming, a concern that threatens the survival of many contemporary institutions?

There are many reasons to be Jewish and many reasons to participate in the life of the organized Jewish community and the life of a synagogue. The most important reasons are those that speak to the individual, because they bring meaning into our lives.

Chapter 8

Leading the Jewish Community into the Future

My teacher Jacob Rader Marcus, longtime professor of American Jewish History at Hebrew Union College–Jewish Institute of Religion, Cincinnati, and founder of the American Jewish Archives, was considered by many Judaic scholars to be the dean of American Jewish history. Some even credit him with establishing American Jewish history as an academic field of inquiry. He often warned his students about the dangers of prophesying the future, suggesting that it was a task best left to the ancient Hebrew prophets. He argued that prophecy was always better evaluated from the perspective of hindsight. Marcus had learned this lesson the hard way. His first book, *The Rise and Destiny of the German Jew,* which optimistically predicted the future of German Jewry, was published in 1934, just as Adolph Hitler rose to power in Germany. Clearly, his predictions about the future of German Jewry were wildly inaccurate. As a result of the destruction of European Jewry during the Holocaust and Marcus's misreading of the trajectory of history, he turned his attention primarily to the United States and exclusively to recording the past rather than predicting the future. Throughout this volume, I have been mindful of the lesson, even if I have chosen not to follow his advice. The current state of the North American Jewish community requires predictions of the future so that people can successfully navigate their way there. The contemporary community requires a major overhaul, some of which I have tried to describe in these pages. I believe that such an overhaul will have to be done speedily. An optimistic Jewish future depends on it.

Among the other charges Marcus gave his students was the directive to bring closer to Judaism as many people as possible. I am sure that this directive emerged as a response to the loss suffered by the Jewish people during World War II. Six million Jews died during the Holocaust. Marcus wanted his students to make up this loss numerically much in the same way he was trying to do so intellectually in his own work. To fulfill Marcus's charge to me, I have to bring people close to Judaism in whatever way possible. But I will do it by allowing Judaism to communicate on its own, rather than manipulating it to do so.

Other Jewish leaders are trying to do things similar to what was being asked of me by Marcus. My colleague, Rabbi Lawrence A. Hoffman, a liturgist and specialist in Jewish worship, argues that Jewish history has entered its third epoch. During the first epoch, asserts Hoffman, Judaism was identified by its limits, articulated in a body of law. During the second epoch, which emerged during the postenlightenment period, science and religion were reconciled. They operated in separate spheres but were not at odds with one another. Religion was not there to answer the questions of science, and science could not be asked to answer the questions posed by religion. This recognition allowed the synagogue to evolve on its own. During the current epoch, we are experiencing an internal revolution, claims Hoffman. In previous generations, people joined synagogues out of a sense of civic obligation. Now the synagogue has to become the place, says Hoffman, where meaning happens. If it is to survive and prosper, the synagogue has to become the place where people find meaning. Hoffman is arguing for a reimagining of the synagogue and its role by developing it into a place where life's big questions are answered and acted upon.

If synagogues are going to regain their rightful place, they will need strong leaders, both clerical and volunteer. These leaders must be willing to implement a new vision for the synagogue. Just as the Jewish community has evolved, so must its leaders, particularly in the synagogue. Like Hoffman, Rabbi Yitz Greenberg also divides Jewish history into three epochs. However, his focus is primarily on institutional leadership rather than the institution itself. Greenberg defines the first epoch of Jewish history as the centuries when Jews were led by the cultic leader, the priest. This role of the priest fit the function of the ancient temple as the Jewish cultic center. During the second epoch, Jews were led by the rabbi, who interpreted the law that governed the community. While most people assume that the destruction of the temple gave rise to the rabbinate, the rabbinate and the synagogue predated the destruction of the temple. However, the struggle over Jewish communal authority became moot once the temple was destroyed. Unlike the priesthood, which was inherited, the rabbinate was open to any male (and eventually females in the liberal denominations). This meant that Jewish leadership was significantly expanded and could be attained by the mastery of sacred texts and Jewish tradition. The third epoch of Jewish history is marked by the leadership dyad of volunteer leader and rabbi. This third epoch was probably provoked by the democratization of the Jewish community and the growth of the Jewish Federation movement as the community's umbrella organization. The Reform movement had already established a partnership between laity and clergy early in its history, and the other denominations were copying the Reform movement's infrastructure model. Historian Ellis Rivkin suggested that leaders and the model of leadership they employed actually shaped individual periods of Jewish history. The Jewish community changed when a new form of leadership usurped the leadership status quo and then led the Jewish people in a different direction. Rivkin argues a point that seems to be counterintuitive. For him, the change from one leadership model to another was a quantum leap. The change in leadership did not *follow* a change in the community's circumstances. While it may have needed a different kind of leader, he argues that a different kind of leader appeared and then took the Jewish enterprise in a new direction.

Like the synagogue, the current leadership model in which the rabbi has hegemony over the ritual aspects of the synagogue but is generally not the CEO of the synagogue enterprise is undergoing significant and rapid change. If the synagogue follows the path I have described in this book, then it is inevitable that the role of the rabbi will also change. Already we see that approximately half of the rabbinic graduates of the main denominational rabbinic training institutions do not serve synagogues. Instead, they lead organizations, teach in educational settings, or provide pastoral counseling, among other things. Some of these rabbinic graduates are intentionally avoiding synagogues that are reticent to change. And many of these newly minted rabbis have become social entrepreneurs, developing their own Jewish communal programs and institutions. It is not hard to imagine that the rabbinate, which became professionalized only in recent history, may once again become avocational, as it was during its incipient stages and into the medieval period. I think that such a change will allow the rabbi to become an independent leader once again, not subject to the whims of a board or congregation.

Similarly, Hillel on college campuses, which might be described as the community and synagogue center of Jewish life on campus, used to have rabbis as their executive directors. Now few rabbis serve as executive directors of such institutions. Instead, Hillels are engaging CEOs, who busy themselves with the business of running the organization so that rabbis can focus their attention on the religious aspects of the enterprise.

It is conceivable that your synagogue may be one of the few religious institutions that will not change but will continue to flourish in the years ahead because a sufficient number of members are willing to support it. But based on what I see happening to synagogues throughout North America, I am willing to prophesy that the majority of synagogues—and other Jewish communal institutions—will undergo significant change during this generation, if they haven't done so already. Such radical change will be necessary for synagogues to successfully evolve so that they can better serve the community. This kind of change will require bold leaders with vision and determination. Some synagogues already have the adaptive leadership necessary to navigate this change. Those that do not have such leaders may not survive. They certainly will not thrive. Some institutions and their leaders are afraid of the trends—and the changes that accompany them—as outlined in this book. Others welcome the opportunity for such change. I am among those who are excited about what the future Jewish community will look like and what it will offer. While we have accomplished a great deal to this point in our history, the best days are yet to come—if we are willing to respond to the challenges set forth in this volume and do the hard work necessary to elevate the synagogue to sacred heights.

Ten Things We Know about Communal and Synagogue Leadership

1. Paraphrasing a rabbinic teaching, "A leader can only take a community where it is prepared to go."
2. Leaders have to lead with vision. Superb skills and effective tactics are necessary complements but insufficient replacements for leadership.
3. Leadership is a strategy. It is not a state of being or a personality trait.
4. Leaders have to be allowed to lead. They can't be bogged down by bureaucratic process or held back by a volunteer board.

5. Leadership transcends the barriers of age. The ability to lead is neither limited by age nor determined by it.
6. Leadership is earned. It is not an entitlement or a designation.
7. Leaders are not afraid to work in partnerships with others, nor are they afraid of others climbing on their shoulders and reaching higher. They are also not afraid that their ideas will be lost through what is now being called Open Source Judaism (anything Jewish that is available for free on the Internet and elsewhere).
8. Leaders are willing to take risks that may uncomfortable for others. As a result, leaders are not afraid of failure.
9. Leaders are not afraid to show others their human vulnerabilities.
10. Leaders want to raise up disciples and are not afraid of losing their role to those whom they have raised up.

Rabbi David Wolpe and Sinai Temple

Many rabbis have provided excellent leadership to their synagogues, and some new alternative structures are certainly built on the vision of their spiritual leaders. But few synagogues have been turned around as a direct result of their leadership. The volunteer leaders of Sinai Temple in Los Angeles believed that only a leader with national prominence could help their synagogue realize its great and unrealized potential. So they sought out such a leader.

Rabbi David Wolpe joined Sinai Temple in Los Angeles as its senior rabbi in 1997. While not the largest of Conservative synagogues in the United States, it has been a high-profile institution for many years, primarily because of the many celebrities and high-profile individuals who call it their synagogue. With more than three hundred staff members and an operating budget of more than $14 million for the synagogue and its Sinai Akiba

Academy, Sinai is a formidable institution. Although he is the son of a rabbi, Wolpe never intended to become a congregational rabbi. Prior to his appointment at Sinai, he was a scholar and lecturer and the author of numerous books. By his own count, he had lectured at more than three hundred congregations and conferences before accepting the position at Sinai. At the same time, he served as assistant to the chancellor at the Jewish Theological Seminary of America (JTS), an academic center of the Conservative movement in New York City, following his tenure in a similar position as special assistant to the president of the University of Judaism (now American Jewish University) in Los Angeles. He continues to write and speak. Wolpe was named the most influential pulpit rabbi in America by *Newsweek* (2012) and among the fifty most influential Jews in the world by the *Jerusalem Post* (2012). He delivered the opening blessing at the Democratic National Convention in 2012, surely a sign of his high profile in the national community.

When Wolpe's predecessor, Rabbi Zvi Dershowitz, retired from Sinai, the synagogue was experiencing many challenges. It had suffered the often abrupt departure of its previous senior rabbis (either by choice or against their will). Its volunteer leaders thought that only a charismatic leader could help turn Sinai around. So they actively pursued Wolpe, sometimes challenging the placement rules of the Rabbinic Assembly, the organization of Conservative rabbis, which required ten years of experience for a rabbi to take on such a large pulpit. Wolpe was known to the congregation, because he had led High Holiday services there, primarily for children, during his days as a student at the University of Judaism. Moreover, some leaders of the congregation knew him from their undergraduate days together at college. To be sure, Wolpe is not a perfect leader. Few people are. While an excellent orator, by his own admission he is not one who gives in to small talk. And some controversial positions he has taken, such as his infamous 2001 Passover sermon in which he challenged the historic validity of the exodus from Egypt, have brought Wolpe and the congregation international attention—not necessarily the kind desired. Sinai is not without its problems. But it remains a significant institution because Rabbi Wolpe is at its helm.

LESSONS LEARNED BY SINAI TEMPLE

1. While visionary leaders can take institutions to places that only they can imagine, these institutions may now be subject to more scrutiny, because it is assumed that that the entire institution has been elevated. Successful leadership alone cannot meet all the challenges a synagogue faces.
2. Succession planning for charismatic leaders is difficult; it may be impossible.
3. Synagogues can hitch themselves to a rising rabbinic star and will, in fact, be elevated in the process.
4. National and international prominence of a leader may force a synagogue out of its comfort zone.
5. Superb current leadership is no guarantee of future success.

Reflection and Discussion Questions for Synagogue Leaders

1. If a synagogue is a system, what does it need to do beyond having one strong leader with international prominence for it to prosper and grow?
2. How does a synagogue know when it is so far beyond a downward spiral that it cannot be saved, even by an exceptionally strong leader?
3. What are the makings of a partnership or leadership team when a strong leader is not available? Can such a team

replace an individual? Can it provide the same direction as a strong leader if the latter is not available?

The Jewish community is not without its potential leaders. However, its structure and its institutions often stymie the expression of leadership by strong individuals. As a result, they may find opportunities to lead outside the community or institution. If we want individuals to lead our community into an optimistic future, then we have to provide them with the support they need to be able to lead effectively. This may require changes in governance and the rebuilding of institutional infrastructures.

Chapter 9

Big Tent Judaism

Big Tent Judaism is a concept developed by the Jewish Outreach Institute, the organization that I am privileged to lead, that reflects the value of pluralism in the Jewish community. I argue that Big Tent Judaism is a foundational value of Judaism and should also be the primary value on which we build up the Jewish community and the synagogue, which have become far too insular and monochromatic. If you don't agree with the status quo, then you are not welcome to participate in its mainstream. I believe that the Jewish communal tent should be big enough to contain those who disagree with one another and yet are also willing to advocate the right of one another to remain inside the tent. While the community has always been diverse, its experience in the contemporary period reflects a diversity never seen before, particularly in North America. For example, there is a growing number of multiracial families as well as families with adult partners who are either gay or lesbian. But sometimes I feel that the support for this diversity, which once animated Judaism, is being stifled, and the community's rich texture is being eaten away as a result. Institutional survivalism is causing Jewish leaders to circle the wagons, making it difficult for those who are different from the status quo to enter. Financial challenges and the maintenance of physical plants is forcing institutions to be risk averse. The current diversity in Jewish life is a result of acculturation, intermarriage, and the adoption of American culture. What takes place in the North American society that surrounds the Jewish community directly affects it. For the synagogue to remain purposeful, it has to provide services and programs that directly address the needs of a diverse population and make room for the various elements that are present in the general Jewish community. Moreover, an inclusive community has to invite civil discourse regarding those principles that could potentially divide it. The continued growth of the Jewish people will be found in diversity, not in uniformity.

If the synagogue is to affirm the values of Big Tent Judaism and secure its future as a result, if the synagogue is to survive, then it has to embrace all these various subgroups without privileging any one of them over the others. This will require more expansive thinking than was common in the past—when the synagogue attempted to simply accommodate the traditional nuclear family—because some of these groups challenge the traditional norms of the community.

Consider, for example, a family that adopts a child in what is called an open adoption, something that is becoming more common. In previous generations, the identity of the birth mother was generally concealed from the adoptive family and almost always from the adopted children. Adopted children were unable to discover anything about their families of origin, since the files about their adoptions—generally held by a family service agency or one specifically dedicated to adoptive services—were legally sealed. It was assumed that such confidentiality would protect the adopted child and his or her family as well as the family of origin. But the rules have changed in many instances. As a result, the birth mother in an open adoption often becomes part of the family unit, participating in the life of the child and the adoptive family. This birth mother may join the family in celebrations as the child marks each life transition. Thus, when a child celebrates a bar or bat mitzvah, the birth mother may want to be involved, and the adoptive family may want to include her in this celebration, as they have in other family experiences. But how will the synagogue respond to her, and to her role whose definition is evolving, especially if she is not Jewish?

A second group that is growing in size and significance in the Jewish community is single mothers by choice, women who have chosen to parent children (often after giving birth to them, although sometimes after adopting or employing surrogate mothers) without a partner or spouse. These women are typically beyond the average U.S. marrying age (about twenty-nine years old) or the average Jewish marrying age (about thirty-five, older than the American average because of the years required to obtain an advanced education). Historically, women who became single mothers (as a result of the death of a partner or divorce) often became socially and economically disenfranchised by Jewish institutions, particularly the synagogue. Generally speaking, however, these women are socially and economically enfranchised, one factor that gives them the opportunity to choose to become mothers without partners. Since the synagogue's focus since World War II has been on families with young children, with the presumption that these families include two parents, programs have not been designed to accommodate single mothers.

When people who are lesbian, gay, bisexual, or transgendered were not welcome in the Jewish community, rather than opting out of synagogue life, many developed their own institutions. Some of the institutions in which they were not welcome now provide opportunities for Jewish life for LGBT community members. As a result, some people who are LGBT have chosen to participate in these synagogues. Others have chosen to remain members of those institutions that have been specifically designed to meet the needs of the LGBT community. However, had synagogues opened their doors early on to this specific group of people, then it is possible that its members would not have developed their own institutions.

We have an opportunity now for synagogues to reflect the diversity of the community and apply the philosophy of Big Tent Judaism, where all are welcome and embraced, irrespective of their subgroups. This approach will serve as a herald to all those who were historically disenfranchised by the organized Jewish community. Individual institutions will have to welcome them. They can start with a big sign on the institution that says, "All are welcome." If they are so inclined, synagogues can specify the target populations.

Ten Working Principles of Big Tent Judaism

1. All people are welcome in an inclusive Jewish community, including those with a diversity of opinions, beliefs, affiliations, levels of observance, and so forth. An inclusive Jewish community is built on a culture of welcoming newcomers.

2. All are welcome in an inclusive Jewish community, regardless of background or status, particularly those who have traditionally been marginalized, such as Jews of color, members of the LGBT community, and those who have intermarried.

3. Participants in an inclusive Jewish community lead with meaning rather than obligation. An inclusive Jewish community provides a benefit to all its participants; that is, they all feel they belong and are at home.

4. An inclusive Jewish community acknowledges that many paths lead a person into the community and that people take different paths once they enter it.

5. An inclusive Jewish community recognizes that Judaism competes with all other options for people's time and

therefore must provide high-quality, meaningful experiences that also answer the big questions they may have about their own life journeys.

6. An inclusive Jewish community identifies and then addresses the obstacles keeping more individuals from participation, such as insider language or the high cost of Jewish life.

7. An inclusive Jewish community takes Jewish life out to where people are, rather than waiting for them to enter Jewish communal institutions, and helps them answer for themselves, why be Jewish?

8. An inclusive Jewish community includes a coalition of organizations that offer the entire gamut of Jewish life and lets the users decide the priorities of the community, rather than each institution trying to be all things to all people.

9. Participants in an inclusive Jewish community are passionately committed to sharing it with newcomers and are willing to work to improve it and nurture its growth for the future.

10. Programs and ideas that work to grow an inclusive Jewish community are open source and shared among all individuals and organizations interested in a more vibrant Judaism and Jewish community.

Nashuva

According to the founder of Nashuva (literally, "let us return"), it is a "soulful community . . . open to all." Nashuva was founded in Los Angeles in 2004 by Rabbi Naomi Levy. According to Levy, who continues as its spiritual leader, Nashuva is a prayer community. Once monthly, it gathers for prayer. And once monthly, it gathers for a service project. These are the functions of

Nashuva—to come together for prayer and for service. According to Rabbi Levy, prayer leads a person to inner peace. But that is insufficient. It must also lead a person to action, to heal this broken world.

Nashuva is diverse, reflecting the ideals of Big Tent Judaism, for it attracts people from all walks of life. While it is still in its incipient stages, Nashuva's leaders do not envision Nashuva as a synagogue. It intentionally has no dues, no membership, and no building and is welcoming to all, irrespective of background or practice. It reaches several hundred people at its monthly services. During a recent service for the High Holidays that was also streamed online, five hundred people attended, but two hundred thousand viewed the service online.

Participants are encouraged to wear white to prayer services to reflect the simplicity of Shabbat, according to Levy. Music is an important component of the prayer experience, as are the new translations of ancient prayers, which Levy edited to ensure they would not be off-putting to interfaith families. While Levy leads each service, the Nashuva band plays an important role in creating the welcoming spiritual atmosphere that Levy seeks to shape. In her words, "This service is for the outsider."[1] Thus, she makes sure that the entire service is transliterated and accessible.

Since Levy is concerned about creating what she calls "a vast umbrella," Nashuva has not yet determined conclusively how it will deal with issues that may compromise her sensibilities as a Conservative rabbi. She may invite colleagues from other denominations to help her transcend those issues and practices in which she herself feels uncomfortable, such as officiating at interfaith weddings, always striving to make all feel welcome.

Nashuva's own principles reflect the goals of Big Tent Judaism:[2]

1. We are diverse and intergenerational.
2. We are welcoming and accepting.

3. We believe in questioning and in critical thinking.
4. We believe in deep, soulful prayer and in a God who is near and hears prayer.
5. We believe in a Judaism that is meaningful, vital, and joyous.
6. We believe that true prayer leads to action.
7. We are passionately committed to social justice and social action.
8. We believe that each human being has a role to play in actively healing our world.
9. We are committed to thoughtful Jewish learning.
10. We believe in taking care of one another and in the power of community.
11. We believe in transformation, in the God-given power to remake our lives and our world.
12. We choose dialogue over dogma, we choose joy over fear.
13. We believe that opportunities for true interfaith partnership can heal the intolerance and fear that threatens to destroy our world.

Lessons Learned by Nashuva

1. There are people seeking a spiritual connection to Judaism who have not found it among the existing options in the organized Jewish community.
2. Curious people may attend a prayer service once. For them to return, the service has to be joyful and uplifting.
3. Although difficult to maintain as groups grow, intimacy is an important value in creating community.
4. There must be immediate access to prayer language so that all participants can be included.
5. A variety of structures for prayer that are alternatives to current synagogue options are needed.

Reflection and Discussion Questions for Synagogue Leaders

1. Can we create an alternative worship experience that highlights these Big Tent Judaism factors without compromising the requirements of Jewish law or the fixed rituals for prayer? If so, what would those experiences look like and have to include?
2. Is it possible to partner with community groups that are offering alternative experiences? If so, what would a synagogue have to do to form such a partnership?
3. What are the ingredients that make a service such as the one offered by Nashuva possible in a synagogue?

Some people worry that encouraging diversity in the Jewish community will water it down. I believe that the future of the North American Jewish community will be found by opening up our borders rather than by circling the wagons. I call this Big Tent Judaism. We must open our doors and our hearts to all those interested in joining our community and participating in it.

Notes

Chapter 2: Turning the Synagogue Inside Out

1. Jeremy S. Morrison, "The Riverway Project: Engaging Adults in their 20s and 30s in the Process of Transforming the Synagogue," Sept 12, 2008, http://www.synagogue3000.org/riverway-project-engaging-adults-their-20s-and-30s-process-transforming-synagogue.

Chapter 5: Don't Forget the Boomers

1. Herbert J. Gans, "Symbolic Ethnicity: The Future of Ethnic Groups and Cultures in America," in *Nationalism: Critical Concepts in Political Science,* ed. John Hutchinson and Anthony D. Smith (London: Routledge, 2000), 4:1225, quoted in Jack Wertheimer, "Whatever Happened to the Jewish People," *Commentary* (June 2006), http://www.commentarymagazine.com/article/whatever-happened-to-the-jewish-people/.
2. Larry Gelman, "Pay It Backward—The Greatest Wealth Transfer in History," HuffPost, November 4, 2008, http://www.huffingtonpost.com/larry-gellman/pay-it-backward--the-grea_b_140530.html.

Chapter 7: Why Be Jewish?

1. Eliyahu Stern, "We Must Have Answers for 'Why Be Jewish?,' " *The Jewish Week,* July 7, 2007.
2. David Wolpe, *Why Be Jewish?* (New York: Henry Holt, 1995), 92.
3. Brant Rosen, "Why Be Jewish? A Sermon for Yom Kippur 5773," *Shalom Rav* (blog), http://rabbibrant.com/2012/09/27/why-be-jewish-a-sermon-for-yom-kippur-5773/.
4. "Moment Asks 35 American Jews Two Big Questions: What does it mean to be a Jew today? What do Jews bring to the world today?," *Moment Magazine,* May 31, 2010.
5. Interview with the author, March 28, 2013.
6. Rex Weiner, "IKAR Looks Forward to Building without Losing Magic," The Jewish Daily Forward website, January 4, 2013, http://forward.com/articles/168454/ikar-looks-to-build-without-losing-magic/.

Chapter 9: Big Tent Judaism

1. Naomi Levy, interview with the author, April 4, 2013.
2. "Nashuva's 13 Principles: What Are We About?" Nashuva website, nashuva.com.